THE COMPLETE GUIDE TO GROWING YOUR OWN FRUITS AND BERRIES

Everything You Need to Know Explained Simply

By Karen Szklany Gault

THE COMPLETE GUIDE TO GROWING YOUR OWN FRUITS AND BERRIES: EVERYTHING YOU NEED TO KNOW EXPLAINED SIMPLY

Gault, Karen Szklany.
  The complete guide to growing your own fruits and berries : everything you need to know explained simply / by: Karen Szklany Gault.
     p. cm.
  Includes bibliographical references and index.
  ISBN-13: 978-1-60138-348-8
  ISBN-10: 1-60138-348-7
  1. Fruit--United States. 2. Berries--United States. I. Title.
  SB354.8.G38 2010
  635--dc22
                         2010032490

Printed in the United States

PROJECT MANAGER: Ben Stearns
PEER REVIEWER: Marilee Griffin
EDITOR: Nicole Orr
EDITORIAL ASSISTANT: Sylvia Maye
INTERIOR DESIGN: Antoinette D'Amore
FRONT COVER DESIGN: Meg Buchner • megadesn@mchsi.com
BACK COVER: Jacqueline Miller • millerjackiej@gmail.com

Printed on Recycled Paper

We recently lost our beloved pet "Bear," who was not only our best and dearest friend but also the "Vice President of Sunshine" here at Atlantic Publishing. He did not receive a salary but worked tirelessly 24 hours a day to please his parents. Bear was a rescue dog that turned around and showered myself, my wife, Sherri, his grandparents Jean, Bob, and Nancy, and every person and animal he met (maybe not rabbits) with friendship and love. He made a lot of people smile every day.

We wanted you to know that a portion of the profits of this book will be donated to The Humane Society of the United States. *–Douglas & Sherri Brown*

The human-animal bond is as old as human history. We cherish our animal companions for their unconditional affection and acceptance. We feel a thrill when we glimpse wild creatures in their natural habitat or in our own backyard.

Unfortunately, the human-animal bond has at times been weakened. Humans have exploited some animal species to the point of extinction.

The Humane Society of the United States makes a difference in the lives of animals here at home and worldwide. The HSUS is dedicated to creating a world where our relationship with animals is guided by compassion. We seek a truly humane society in which animals are respected for their intrinsic value, and where the human-animal bond is strong.

Want to help animals? We have plenty of suggestions. Adopt a pet from a local shelter, join The Humane Society and be a part of our work to help companion animals and wildlife. You will be funding our educational, legislative, investigative and outreach projects in the U.S. and across the globe.

Or perhaps you'd like to make a memorial donation in honor of a pet, friend or relative? You can through our Kindred Spirits program. And if you'd like to contribute in a more structured way, our Planned Giving Office has suggestions about estate planning, annuities, and even gifts of stock that avoid capital gains taxes.

Maybe you have land that you would like to preserve as a lasting habitat for wildlife. Our Wildlife Land Trust can help you. Perhaps the land you want to share is a backyard— that's enough. Our Urban Wildlife Sanctuary Program will show you how to create a habitat for your wild neighbors.

So you see, it's easy to help animals. And The HSUS is here to help.

THE HUMANE SOCIETY
OF THE UNITED STATES.

2100 L Street NW • Washington, DC 20037 • 202-452-1100
www.hsus.org

TRADEMARK DISCLAIMER

All trademarks, trade names, or logos mentioned or used are the property of their respective owners and are used only to directly describe the products being provided. Every effort has been made to properly capitalize, punctuate, identify, and attribute trademarks and trade names to their respective owners, including the use of ® and ™ wherever possible and practical. Atlantic Publishing Group, Inc. is not a partner, affiliate, or licensee with the holders of said trademarks.

ACKNOWLEDGMENTS

There is a large crowd of people to thank for this book becoming a physical reality. The very first person is my supportive editor, Nicole Orr of Atlantic Publishing Group, who knew I had it in me and kept me going with generous helpings of encouragement. She believed in my ability to carry through to fruition a unique and complete guide to growing your own fruits and berries. Ben Stearns took on editing the final revisions of the book and also deserves my appreciation for his eleventh-hour support. Meg Buchner and her layout team worked their magic to make the book beautiful and ready to print. My husband Edward held down the fort and prepared his share of family dinners, and my daughter Cosette drew lots of lovely pictures for me as I worked at the computer around the clock, wrestling all these words about gardening onto the following pages. My case study contributors shared generously with me their wealth of gardening-related wisdom, hands-on demonstrations, and photographs: Steen Bentzen, Carla Montague, Bill Murphy, Ralph "Chick" Papile, Ken Porter, Becky Pulito of Camelot Cohousing, Jeff Richards, Yvonne Scott, Connie Stanfield, and Roger Swain. Others who contributed photographs, resource referrals, and hands-on help include Beezy Bentzen, Christina Buajila, Mariama Congo, Sarah Florreich, Edward S. Gault, Matthew Higgins, Lucia Papile, Sarah Twichell, and Matt Waugh. Sukey Price, the librarian at Tower Hill Botanical Garden, helped me find some key sources for my research and kept renewing them for as long as I needed them. Finally, no author stands alone, without the help of community, and I am no exception. All my writing companions at the Boston Public Library have become like family to me and deserve my deepest appreciation for all their inspiration and support along the path to my becoming a published author: Alistair Allen, Ann Crotty, Helena Findeisen, Janet Getchall, Andrea Lyon, Fran Majusky, Melita Nasca, Rob Russell, Wayne Soini and Nancy Winter. Other supportive communities that have contributed to the energy and faith it has taken to complete this monumental project include the Bagel Bards, Paulist Center (Catholic) Community, Open Bark Poetry, Out of the Blue Art Gallery, Stone Soup Poetry, Summer Acoustic Music Week community, and John Dillon's online 20/20 Creativity Practice group. Finally, I am deeply grateful to all my neighbors at Mosaic Commons cohousing community in Berlin, Massachusetts (**www.mosaic-commons.org**), who have offered a deep well of ongoing support and patience throughout all the stages of writing this book. It is a community of heart and soul, my home, and the place I am able to do the work of growing my own fruits and berries.

DEDICATION

This book is dedicated to my grandmother, Lucy Rose Szklany, who cultivated my lifelong love of gardening, and to my grandfather, Albin A. Szklany Sr., who always picked the first tomato of the season and washed it with the garden hose just for me.

TABLE OF CONTENTS

INTRODUCTION **13**

Chapter 1: Types of Fruits and Berries **17**

Fruits and Berries Across the Country 17

Geographical Regions of the United States 19

    Pacific Ocean *22*

    Mountains *25*

    Southwest *26*

    Plains *28*

    South Central *29*

    Southeast *30*

    Mid-Atlantic *31*

    Great Lakes *32*

    New England *34*

Chapter 2: What Types of Fruits and Berries
        Should I Grow? **37**

Things to Consider 40

    Topography — lay of the land and soil erosion *40*

    Soil quality *41*

    Moisture *42*

    Climate that supports certain fruits and berries *43*

    Sunlight and shade — what is available for growing *44*

    Pollination opportunities for growth and fruiting success ... *45*

    Available space — how much of each fruit can be planted *47*

    Disease and insect resistance — the survival of fruits and berries ... *48*

Underground structural obstacles 49

Best Seasons 49

Planting seasons 51

Harvesting 51

Some Final Notes about Personal Preference............................53

Chapter 3: Soil Texture, Quality, and Enrichment............57

Soil Testing..58

Acid vs. Alkaline..60

Types of Soil..62

Sandy soil 64

Gravelly Soil 65

Silty soil... 65

Clay soil... 66

Chalky soil.. 66

Peaty soil.. 67

Loamy Soil.. 67

Creating Organic Soil with Worms...68

Why use worms?... 68

Where to find the worms 69

Where to keep the worms.. 70

Furnishing a home for the worms 70

Care of the worms 71

Case Study: A Bin of Worms Named "Steve"........................... 72

Feeding Your Soil 74

Mulch materials for fertile soil... 74

Manures 79

Compost 79

Natural soil composition 82

Layering of soil with mulch materials...................................... 85

*Case Study: Down and Dirty Methods for
Making Garden Soil Fertile* 86

Chapter 4: Basic Gardening Tools You Will Need 89

Description of Tools 89

Clothing *90*

Mapping the garden *92*

Digging and soil preparation *94*

Moving rocks and large piles of earth *96*

Sowing and planting *97*

Containers *98*

Pruning *103*

Protection from pests and diseases *106*

Harvesting equipment *106*

Care and Maintenance of Gardening Tools
for the Winter Months 107

Chapter 5: Pollination **109**

Anatomy of a Fruit Flower 112

Self-Pollinating Plants 113

Cross-Pollinating Plants 114

Artificial Pollination 115

Keeping Bees...118

Chapter 6: Cultivation and Planting...........................**123**

Grafting 125

Planting Tree Fruits 127

Planting Citrus Fruits...132

Planting Melons 137

Planting Brambles 140

Steps to take before planting *141*

Discerning the best brambleberry to grow *142*

Preparing to transplant brambles *143*

Digging the holes for brambles *143*

Completing the planting process *145*

Planting Bush Berries 145

Blueberries *147*

Other bush berries *151*

Planting Strawberries..154

Sunlight *155*

Soil... *156*

Runner production and spacing........................... *156*

Planting *158*

Planting Grape Vines 161

Location *162*

Preparing the soil... *163*

Planting the grape vines...................................... *163*

Trellis design *165*

Vine training systems *168*

Planting Kiwifruit 169

Planting Rhubarb 172

**Chapter 7: Container Gardening and
         Greenhouse Growing**..............................**177**

Container Gardening 178

Types of containers and what they are used for........... *180*

Container planting.. *183*

Sources for obtaining containers............................ *184*

Spaces to put the containers *184*

Case Study: Outrageous Gardening with Recycled Materials........... *186*

Greenhouse Growing..187

Greenhouse design and construction...................... *189*

Heating equipment.. *191*

Fruits and berries that are grown in a greenhouse *192*

Case Study: Raising Tomatoes from Seedlings in Greenhouses........... *193*

Chapter 8: Ongoing Care **197**

General Care 197

Sunlight.. *198*

Watering.. *198*

Fertilizing.. *199*

Weeding... *199*

Pruning.. *200*

*Case Study: Caring for Fruit Trees and Berry Bushes
as a Labor of Love* *204*

Low-Temperature Climate Care 205

Dormancy..206

Protection from frost 207

Chapter 9: Pests and Diseases..................................211

Purchasing Healthy Cultivars 211

Pests 212

Aphids..214

Borers 216

Caspid bugs...217

Caterpillars...218

Curculio 219

Grubs 219

Maggots..220

Mealybugs..221

Repelling mealybugs...221

Mites...222

Moths 223

Nematodes 224

Pear psylla..225

Scale insects..225

Slugs...226

Suckers 227

Wasps 227

Worms..228

General long-term pest protection...229

Barriers for keeping out furry scavengers......................................230

Diseases...230

Common causes..230

Common types of diseases 232

Examples of common fruit plant diseases......................................233

Chapter 10: Enjoying the Feast —
Harvesting and Storing Your Fruit..................241

The Right Time for Harvesting Tree Fruit and Berries.................241

Problems with harvesting too early...242

Problems with harvesting too late 243

Methods for picking fruits and berries 244

The best way to pick each type of fruit 244

CaseStudy: Harvesting, Baking, and Preserving Rabbiteye Blueberries in North Carolina 245

Eat, Drink, and Save Some for Later 250

Appendix A: Resources for Finding Garden Tools and Supplies 251

Appendix B: Recipes 263

Apple Salsa (Matt Higgins) 263

Blueberry Squares (Connie Stanfield) 264

Classic Spanish Sparkling Sangría 264

Fruit Shakes 265

Honey Madelines (a nod to the bees) 266

Hot Apple Soup 267

Lemon Mousse 269

Raspberry Fool 270

Strawberries in Cream 271

Apple Pie 272

Four Berry Fruit Cobbler 273

Grilled Peaches with Cinnamon Sugar Butter 274

Easy Triple Fruit Jam 275

French Cream Fruit Dip 276

Appendix C: List of Scientific Names of Fruits and Berries 277

Glossary 279

Author Biography 283

Index 285

INTRODUCTION

Ever since I was a little girl, I have loved to dig in the earth. I loved to kneel in the grass to plant the seeds, water the growing plants with our garden hose, and pick the food that I grew. My grandmother had the original green thumb of the family, and gardening was one of my favorite things to do with her. I dug, weeded, pruned, and watered with her weekly. When the time was right for harvesting, the peaches smelled and tasted like the sun that kissed them. The raspberries, blackberries, and blueberries melted in my mouth. The peaches made a scrumptious snack at any time of a summer day. The berries made it into salads — if they made it into the kitchen at all. Sometimes, I was able to wait long enough to eat them topped with fresh whipped cream. The memory of how strawberries taste dipped in chocolate has inspired me to try growing them, too. The scent of Concord grapes is downright intoxicating to me, and the generosity of one former employer who let me pick them from the courtyard trellises inspires me to make plans for building my own small arbor.

Are there any gardening memories from your childhood that linger and make you smile? They may be the biggest inspiration for trying to turn a plot of land close to your home into a garden of fresh fruit to pick and eat. You may know children who would delight in helping you plant, nurture, and pick fresh fruit. Your senses may already anticipate the smell and taste of delicious salads, pies, jams, mousses, and salsas that you can make from them. I have written this book to share with you my passion for growing fruits and berries, and to give you the information you need to make your own gardening dreams come true.

Some of the classifications for the food you eat might surprise you. One example is that nuts are considered a tree fruit by some botanists. Grapes are considered berries. This book is full of delicious details that will light the fire of your deepest, earthiest side. Dig down and decide which fruits and berries are truly *your* favorites. Which ones give you the most pleasure to taste? Which ones do you dream of walking outside to pick and take that first juicy bite of? Then, decide which patch of land outside your door is the sunniest and start planning where to put them in that sacred plot of earth.

Once you determine which fruits you are yearning to grow first, it is time to measure the plot of land you have designated as your fruit garden. This includes determining what architectural features of your home and yard space you will adorn with fruit, such as porches, patios backyard space, and front yard space. If you live in the city, you will need to use your yard space differently, or adorn a balcony or a window box instead of a yard, porch, or patio. If the latter is true, it is possible that there are community gardening spaces for you to rent or barter with neighbors for. Perhaps there is an elderly neighbor who would take delight in your gardening efforts. There may also be a neighborhood gardening club that you might like to join. There is nothing like a sense of community to keep you going, even if you prefer to be a lone gardener who enjoys the plants themselves as company most of the time. If there is no soil that is healthy enough for planting directly into, you can create raised beds or grow some of your fruits in a variety of containers, or both. No matter what you have at your fingertips, or feet, you will be able to transform that place into a garden that brings you peace, happiness, and a mouthful of sweetness.

In order to complete all the gardening tasks involved, you will need to know which tools to use and at which stage you will first need them. *Chapter 4 gives you this information and offers suggestions for places to obtain those tools and how to take good care of them.* In addition to my sun hat and gardening gloves, my favorite tools are the trowel and hand fork. They help me with digging and weeding small patches of earth while I am sitting or kneeling on the ground. I also love to water with the garden hose, which has a spray nozzle at the head of it. When I was little, the rainbows that formed while I gave my plants their daily drink of water were magical to me.

After you have those plants firmly rooted in the ground and drinking up the sunshine and water in your garden, it will be time to relax before you head back out to your garden to give your new plants the extra care they need to keep growing strong. By the end of the summer, you will be able to sit down to delicious food made with the fruits of a season of your efforts — Appendix B is filled with some of my favorite recipes for you to try.

photo by Herb Stanfield

CHAPTER 1

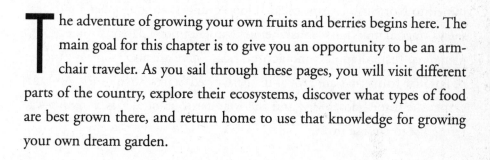

Types of Fruits and Berries

The adventure of growing your own fruits and berries begins here. The main goal for this chapter is to give you an opportunity to be an armchair traveler. As you sail through these pages, you will visit different parts of the country, explore their ecosystems, discover what types of food are best grown there, and return home to use that knowledge for growing your own dream garden.

FRUITS AND BERRIES ACROSS THE COUNTRY

Our explorations lead us to discover that there are hundreds of fruits and berries that are grown across the world. There are more than 50 species of fruits and berries native to North America. These include pome fruits, stone fruits, and berries that grow on brambles. Examples of fleshy pome fruits that grow on trees and contain small seeds for their reproduction are apples, crabapples, pears, and quinces. Stone fruits also grow on trees and contain hard pits inside them, such as apricots, cherries, peaches, and plums. Brambles are thorny bushes that grow berries, such as raspberries and blackberries. Berries that grow on bushes instead of brambles include blueberries, cranberries, currants, mulberries, and strawberries. Then there are fruit species that have been introduced from Mediterranean and Subtropical countries such as Spain, Greece, Algeria, Turkey, and South Africa, which together amount to more than 40 types of fruits and berries that have been introduced and have adapted to living in the United States. Included in this migration have been avocados, palm dates, figs, grapes, kumquats, guavas, passion fruits, pomegranates, and peanuts. Citrus fruits such as lemons, limes, oranges, and grapefruit have been brought to North America from tropical areas such as Mexico, Central America, the Caribbean, the South Pacific, Israel, and Egypt. Others that have grown accustomed to North American soil are blood oranges, almonds, betel nuts, cashews, macadamia nuts, muskmelons (cantaloupes), papayas, pineapples, plantains, custard apples, and acai berries. There are also tropical varieties of familiar fruits that are grown in the United States, such as the Amazon grape, the Cape gooseberry, and the Mandarin orange. It is a mouth-watering list to choose from.

You might have already determined what your favorite fruits and berries are. If that is true, the next step is to determine the growing conditions that are necessary for them to yield their best fruits. Each type of fruit and berry requires a specific type of climate for its survival, flowering, and fruit production. The climate that supports specific fruits, nuts, and berries does so because it affects the conditions of the soil under which the trees, brambles, bushes, and vines that produce them have spread their roots. The animals, insects, and other critters that live in an ecosystem depend upon the fruits, nuts, and berries that grow there. An ecosystem is a community of animals, trees, plants, insects, and other creatures that live in a particular geographic area of the world that experiences a particular type of climate, or weather pattern. The honeybee, for example, is one of the most important insects to humans worldwide, because they pollinate the flowers that produce 80 percent of the food people eat. Also, the nectar they collect is used to produce a tasty, healing elixir. Pet rabbits and cats enjoy nibbling on domestically grown strawberries, and wild birds such as crows, woodpeckers, catbirds, and wild turkeys depend upon wild strawberries that grow in the forest. Gray squirrels tend to sample both varieties because they are at home in both types of habitat. The domestic garden and woodland forest represent two different types of ecosystems that may be in close proximity to one another but can still support similar animal and insect species.

GEOGRAPHICAL REGIONS OF THE UNITED STATES

Different ecosystems present specific types of landscapes that support particular varieties of fruits, nuts, and berries. Some of those landscapes are wetter than others. For example, woodland forests and rainforests are wetter than deserts. A meadow retains moisture, but it is exposed to more direct sunlight than the floor of a forest. They each host different types of plants and animals.

Different varieties of the same type of fruit grow on different types of landscapes because one might grow better in a different type of soil than another. Each has its own requirement for the necessary amount of direct sunlight and moisture, can withstand different temperature ranges, and produces fruit on its own schedule. For example, June-bearing strawberries require more direct sunlight and produce a single crop of fruit early in the summer, but day-neutral strawberries are tolerant of more shade and produce fruit from early spring through late summer. You have a broader choice of garden terrain for growing the day-neutral variety successfully. Muscadine grapes require a lighter, sandier soil and the warm, sunny climate of the southeastern states. They can be damaged by temperatures below 0 degrees Fahrenheit. Concord grapes grow most abundantly in dark, moist soil. They are better adapted to cooler temperatures and are more successfully grown in the Northeastern states.

The list of fruits and berries in this chapter is presented according to the region of the United States in which they are most prolific. Those of you who do not live in the United States can compare your climate to one of these regions to determine which cultivar will produce most abundantly in your back yard. A cultivar is a seedling that is cut from a particular variety of fruit tree or berry plant and re-rooted for the purpose of transplanting to a home garden. They are usually developed in a greenhouse at a nursery.

In the following sections, you will find information about fruits in different categories, such as common tree fruits, citrus fruits, brambles, bushes, vine fruits, melons, and exotic fruits, such as kiwis. Tree fruits are fruits that are produced by flowers that grow on trees. They grow, flower, and produce fruit in a specific type of climate. For example, citrus trees grow best in a temperate or tropical climate, such as that found in Florida or California. Apples, pears, and plums are more prolific in cooler regions of the country, such as New England.

Tree nuts are also considered fruits because they are produced by trees. They are a combination of seed and fruit. Walnuts grow best on mountainous terrain along the north Atlantic coast and the Appalachian Mountains located inland along the Mid-Atlantic states. Macadamia nuts are adapted better to tropical climates, such as Hawaii. Pecans grow more abundantly in the forests of Georgia and North Carolina.

Brambles are another fruit category. A bramble is a perennial berry bush with thorny canes that grow erect, arching, or prostrate. The term perennial refers to plants and flowers that grow back each year. The cane of a bramble is the stalk that produces the buds from which fruit develops.

Some grow close to the ground as runners, and can be trained on a trellis like a vine. The runners are the offspring produced by the parent cane after the completion of the fruiting season. It is the part of the plant used for cultivating new plants that will be grown elsewhere, such as in a pot. The most common examples of brambles are the raspberry and blackberry.

Types of fruit and their characteristics

Types of Fruit	Characteristics	Examples
Tree fruit Citrus Pome Tree Nut	Grow from trees that produce blossoms; grown from a cultivar Grow in warm climates Contain a stone Nuts that grow on trees	Apple, Pear, Peach, Cherry, Plum Grapefruit, Lemon, Lime Peach, Plum, Cherry Walnut, Pecan, Almond, Macadamia
Brambles	Grow thorny canes Perennial (grow back each year)	Blackberry Raspberry
Bush Berries	Berries that grow on bushes	Blueberry Currant Cranberry Gooseberry Strawberry
Vine fruit	Fruit that grow on vines	Grapes, Melons
Tropical	Grow in tropical countries in very moist soil	Avocado, Pineapple, Kiwi

Some fruits are crossovers between two of these groupings, such as cantaloupes, which grow on vines but are considered melons. Grapes grow on vines but are considered berries, because some of the types of vines they grow on may be classified as canes, and they often develop runners that are cultivated for new growth. The grapes themselves are harvested and used as berries, such as for juices, jams, and preserves. This is especially true for the Concord grape variety.

There are two types of climates that will be discussed in this book: macroclimates and microclimates. Macroclimate refers to the overall climate, or weather pattern, of a particular geographic region of the world. Microclimate refers to the variations in climate that affect a smaller area of land within a larger geographic region, such as an ecosystem. *Microclimates will be discussed in greater detail in Chapter 2.* This chapter will focus on the macroclimate of the major regions of the United States. Not all geographers and cartographers (mapmakers) agree on which states belong to which regions, particularly when there are landscapes in those states that belong to two separate regions, such as the mountains to the north and deserts to the southwest of Nevada. They have been grouped together in this book according to the features that they share: landscape, weather patterns, and ecosystems that support the fruits, nuts, and berries reported to grow best in that part of the country. The United States is the main focus for the organization of this chapter, and the book as a whole. Those who live in other countries, and on other continents, may be able to compare the information contained in these pages to the climate patterns of their home country and find this information useful.

Pacific Ocean

Washington, Oregon, Alaska, California, and Hawaii are the Pacific states. One geographical feature that they all share is the Pacific Ocean. Along the shoreline, rock and sand are the predominant terrain. The ocean waves crawl inland at high tide to water the plants that grow there. Palms trees are tall and strong, so they are able to withstand the attacks of ocean gales and tropical storms. They thrive in climates that range from arid to temperate, where the temperature does not fall below 30 degrees Fahrenheit, and populate the shorelines of Southern California and Hawaii. The variety of fruit that they produce includes coconuts, dates, and acai berries. One nut tree that grows best on the coastline of the Northern Pacific states is the hardy pecan. More rain falls in these areas, which is necessary for palm trees, because the sand that they stand in does not retain water very well. Birds such as gulls, sandpipers, pelicans, and plovers land on the shoreline to feed on tropical sea grapes, gooseberries, currants, thornless huckleberries, blackberries, and raspberries when they are not digging in the mudflats for crustaceans. Native tribes rely on the berries for jams, jellies, concentrates, juices, and syrup.

If you travel inland through the Northern Pacific states of Washington, Oregon, Northern California, and Southeast Alaska, the climate is usually cool and rainy, and the temperature does not normally drop below 0 degrees Fahrenheit. The soil is more rich and moist, and supports tree fruits that tolerate the cooler temperatures, such as apple, peach, pear, plum, tart and sweet cherry, melon, and rhubarb. The hybrid chestnut and the walnut are nut trees that bear a larger crop in this region, because they share a similar need for moisture. The tougher varieties of berries, such as strawberry, blueberry, currant, gooseberry, lingonberry, blackberry, raspberry, bunch grapes, and hardy kiwi fruit will grow in this region. Misty, northern boreal forests host these fruits, and the animals that depend on them. Black bears, otters, deer, wolves, and eagles are some of the animals that depend upon the berries and tree fruit found in these forests.

The temperature in the mountains of inland Washington, Oregon, and Alaska dips as low as 40 degrees below zero Fahrenheit, and the wind adds to the chill. The terrain is mainly rocky, with grasses growing between the stepping-stones. Only the hardiest of fruit and nut trees will live and produce if they are grown there. Such tree fruits are hardy apple, hardy pear, European plum, and plants grown to maturity in containers. The butternut is the only type of nut tree that holds up against the extreme climate. The Alpine variety of strawberry is best suited to grow in the mountains. Other berries that have also grown in mountain terrain include the black-berry, raspberry, half-high blueberry, currant, gooseberry, and lingonberry. These fruits have become acclimated to the cold temperatures and are able to receive enough warmth from the sun to feed their growth and flower-ing, and eventually their production of a fruit crop. Black bears, grizzly bears, and the Kodiak bears of Alaska are famous for feeding on berries, particularly those that grow on brambles. They also eat acorns, pecans, and walnuts. When there is no immediate prey for an eagle or hawk to capture, they will grab a ripe, fleshy fruit such as an apple, pear, or plum with their beak and eat it. Because of the limited choice of fruit that can be grown successfully in the ground, those who enjoy living in the moun-tains often choose to grow a more diverse selection of their favorites in containers or greenhouses. *More about this method of growing will be dis-cussed in Chapter 7.*

The Hawaiian islands and most of the Pacific states have an area of tropical rainforest climate. The temperature ranges between 64 and 80 degrees Fahrenheit and the air stays warm and humid. It never freezes and there is plenty of sunshine. Rain falls often and drains the clay soil of nutrients, but it is built back up by the dropped fruits and leaves of a variety of fruit plants, so the fruits that are borne on the trees that flourish there grow plump, juicy, and sweet. Citrus fruits, such as oranges, grapefruits, limes, and lemons grow abundantly in these forests because of the high humidity that keeps the soil perpetually moist. Other tropical fruits that also grow in this environment are avocados, bananas, plantains, mangos, papayas, guavas, and pineapples. Nuts supported by the climate include cashews, macadamia nuts, peanuts, nutmegs, and coconuts. Wild, tropical varieties of all the types of berries mentioned also grow there, such as gooseberries, brambles, and grapes.

Along with the trees, the rainforest supports a diverse collection of creatures that find those fruits, nuts, and berries scrumptious. The most prolific species in the rainforest are the insects, such as ants, butterflies, beetles, caterpillars, and dragonflies. They are good at helping fallen fruits and leaves decompose so that they feed the continued growth and production of the edibles on the trees that live there. They also feed the birds that

photo by Matt Higgins

populate the forest, such as parrots, macaws, eagles, kingfishers, cuckoos, and toucans. Several different types of bees call the rainforest home while they keep the trees pollinated throughout the year. Monkeys, sloths, and bats are the mammals that happily inhabit the rainforest and like to eat the fruit. The conditions of the rainforest can be imitated by maintaining a greenhouse if the fruit that grows there are among your favorites. *This type of growing is also covered in Chapter 7.*

Mountains

The Mountain states are Arizona, Colorado, Idaho, Montana, Nevada, New Mexico, Utah, and Wyoming. This ecosystem hosts streams and rivers, which flow through the mountains toward the lakes and deserts. The winter months are few and mild, and the summers are sunny, hot, and dry. The soil at the higher elevations absorbs more moisture because that is where more of the rain falls. Therefore, the mountainous terrain supports more fruits, nuts, and berries. Tree fruits that grow and produce in the mountains include apple, pear, plum, cherry, and the butternut. Rhubarb also grows there. Berry varieties that can be found on this terrain include the day-neutral strawberry, blackberry, raspberry, half-high blueberry, currant, lingonberry, and hardy bunch grapes. Among the animals that call the mountain states home, wild cats, wolves, moose, gophers, and squirrels are a few that feast on the fruit that grows there. If you live in the mountains of any of these states, you may have seen a deer or a moose saunter through your backyard to nibble on a snack.

At the bottom of the mountains, the predominant landscape is the sandy, arid desert. It is home to armadillos, lizards, prairie dogs, snakes, hummingbirds, bats, owls, frogs, toads, hawks, and roadrunners. This distinction applies more to Arizona, Nevada, and New Mexico than the other mountain states. The southern halves of these states are also considered part of the region known as the Southwest. Container gardening is prevalent among the residents of this region, and gives the grower more control of the soil in which the fruit and berry trees are planted and grown. The fruits grown in containers could be placed around the native cacti in unique arrangements.

Southwest

The Southwest region includes the states of Arizona and New Mexico. It also includes Texas as well as the desert regions of Southern California, Nevada, and Utah. The climate is dry and hot and the temperature does not drop below 20 degrees Fahrenheit. Trees that do not need low temperatures to reach dormancy can survive the warm winter and produce more abundantly in this region. These are known as "low-chill" trees. Hardier varieties would not survive here, because they require the lower temperatures to enter their dormant state for their winter chill protection. It is part of their life cycle that contributes to their productivity. The low-chill varieties of tree fruit species that grow in the Southwest are apples, sweet and sour cherries, peaches, pears, plums, and melons (bordering California). If you want to grow nuts, you may choose from Carpathian walnut, hickory, and filbert. Berries that may grow in the Southwest are the day-neutral strawberry, blackberry, low-chill kiwifruit, and grapes. There exists more diversity in growing possibilities on this terrain than the term desert implies, which is especially true of the greener canyon lands of Southern Nevada and West Texas, such as El Paso, where the Rio Grande provides a source of irrigation. There is also diversity in the species of critters that scurry along or soar above the desert floor to feast on the food that grows there. These include armadillos, herons, prairie dogs, hummingbirds, coyotes, owls, hawks, ravens, bats, porcupines, scorpions, tarantulas, snakes, lizards, and beetles. Those who live in the more arid desert regions of the

Southwestern states often rely on container gardening to grow their fruits and berries. The sandy quality of the soil does not support most fruit trees and berry plants, and extreme heat and wind conditions make it necessary to move the plants indoors to protect them. Muscadine grapes are most tolerant to relatively high alkalinity in the soil, so the sand would be of benefit to them. They will need to be watered often though, so they may benefit from being grown in raised beds and trained on a trellis in an area that does not receive the full force of the desert wind.

Plains

Also referred to as the Midwestern states, the Central Plains states include North Dakota, South Dakota, Ohio, Illinois, Indiana, Kansas, Kentucky, Minnesota, Missouri, and Nebraska. The states listed contain other landscape features, such as mountains and forests. These are the states where the dry, dusty wind whips over the prairies, and miles of flat plains present the predominant landscape for growing any crop, including fruits and berries. The climate is similar to the desert, but colder, and a little greener. In winter, the temperature falls as low as -20 degrees Fahrenheit and the summers are sunny, hot, and dry. Because of the temperature and other climate extremes, only hardy varieties of tree fruit species have grown and produced successfully on the plains of the Midwest. These include apples, pears, peaches, plums, apricots, and tart cherries. Nuts that may be grown there are

walnuts, hardy filberts, and hickories. Berries that grow there are strawberries, brambles, currants, gooseberries, lingonberries, bunch grapes, and hardy kiwifruits. Then there is the versatile rhubarb, which is not in either category. In addition to humans, animals also enjoy feasting on these fruits, nuts, and berries. The most adorable visitor might be the prairie dogs. Other animals that enjoy the fruits, nuts, and berries that are often found on the plains include eagles, bats, frogs, hummingbirds, horses, snakes, jackrabbits, deer, coyotes, and bears. At dusk in the summer, the fireflies take their turn.

South Central

The South Central states that have not been mentioned in any of the other above categories are Arkansas, Louisiana, Mississippi, and Oklahoma. The eastern part of Texas also has some of the same terrain common to these states. Although this region is in the southern portion of the country, inland temperatures can still drop to as low as 10 degrees Fahrenheit, particularly closer to the plains. The terrain at the border of the Gulf of Mexico is milder and friendlier to growing fruits, nuts, and berries. The soil retains moisture and provides more nutrients to trees and plants. The lowest temperature of 54 degrees Fahrenheit usually occurs in January. July is the warmest month, with a high of 82 degrees Fahrenheit. Tree fruits that are most prolific in the South Central states include low-chill apples, peaches, sweet and sour cherries, pears, and plums. Melons also grow and produce well in these states. Nut trees often found in this region include hybrid chestnuts, walnuts, and hardy pecans. Berries that grow in this region are day-neutral strawberries, blackberries, rabbiteye blueberries, and muscadine grapes. The rabbiteye blueberries also produce well in the Southeastern states, because both regions border the Gulf of Mexico. That blueberry variety grows best in the moist soil of the warmer states. Closer to the Gulf, the climate approaches the subtropical and fruits, such as pineapples and mangos, grow in the wild. The honey bee is honored as the "state insect" for all four of these states, which is very important to those who love to breathe in the fragrance of flowers and eat freshly picked food.

The animals that live in the South Central states depend on the fruits and berries that grow there, and create a demand that is met with an ample supply. Part of this is due to their habits. The state animal of Louisiana is the Louisiana Black Bear; for Mississippi and Arkansas it is the white-tailed deer. Both animals live among trees and eat the berries. The bears have a tendency to break off the branches from which they eat the berries, or feed their cubs with them. The deer also eat the leaves. These actions are a form of pruning that result in the berry bushes growing back each year. The state bird for Louisiana is the brown pelican, which feasts on berries when it spends time ashore. For Mississippi and Arkansas, the state bird is the mockingbird, which lives in trees and also feasts on berries, nuts, and seeds. All of these animals depend in some way on the fruit trees to give them shade and protection from predators. The trees depend on the abundance of moisture provided by the Gulf of Mexico for their growth and production.

Southeast

photo by Matt Higgins

Alabama, Florida, Georgia, South Carolina, and Tennessee are some examples of Southeastern states. Bordering the Gulf of Mexico along with the South Central states is Florida. With the Southern Atlantic waters to the East of these states, the prevailing climate of the Southeastern United States is tropical. Trees and plants that love rich, moist, warm soil produce harvests of plenty to eat and bake. Florida is well known as a source of citrus fruits that are high in Vitamin C, which is useful during the winter months when residents of the Northeastern states need them most. Among those tree fruits are the oranges (including mandarins), lemons, grapefruits, and limes. Melons, such as cantaloupes and watermelons, also like the rich tropical soil of the Southeastern states.

The Appalachian Mountains also run through some of the Southeastern states. In the mountains, the temperature can dip as low as 20 degrees Fahrenheit in the winter. That is the terrain where some of the trees more suited to cooler climates are found, such as the apples, pears, plums, and pecans. The berries used for salads, pies, and preserves in the deep South states are strawberry, blackberry, rabbiteye blueberry, and muscadine grapes. The state fruit for Georgia is the peach, and the most prolific nut of that state is the peanut. Wild alpine strawberries, blackberries, and huckleberries grow at the higher altitudes, too. Such fruits make these states hospitable to animals such as otters, bears, wolves, rabbits, squirrels, and some turtles. Birds that feast on fruit and insects in Florida and its neighboring states include mockingbirds, owls, egrets, storks, warblers, blackbirds, and kites, which also feed on the ever present ants.

Mid-Atlantic

The Mid-Atlantic region is also referred to as the Eastern Seaboard. The states considered part of this group are Pennsylvania, New Jersey, Delaware, Maryland, Washington, D.C., Virginia, North Carolina, and West Virginia. The Atlantic Ocean influences the climate of the states that border it. Sea grapes and wild brambles might be the only fruit found growing on the sand along the boardwalk, attractive to gulls and other shore birds. Inland, the Appalachian Mountains continue to dominate the terrain, which is hospitable to hardy tree fruits, such as apples, peaches, pears, and European plums, as well as berries like wild brambles and strawberries. Other landscape features of these states are valleys, forests, plains, rivers, and lakes. Lower elevations, such as valleys and plains, are friendlier to apricots, tart cherries, hardy kiwifruit, rhubarb, and even pineapples. Pineapples have been a symbol of welcome along the Atlantic coastline since the beginning of American colonial history. Highbush blueberries, brambles, currants, gooseberries, and bunch grapes are most likely found in the forests and by rivers and lakes. Overall, the climate is subtropical to temperate, and the thermometer usually does not read below 0 degrees Fahrenheit. There is seldom frost damage to worry about, but the wind may damage trees if other types of tree growth, such as evergreens, do not protect them.

Great Lakes

The states that border the Great Lakes are Illinois, Indiana, Ohio, Pennsylvania, Wisconsin, Michigan, Minnesota, and New York. Inclusion of some of these states may relate to the rivers that empty from basins located within their boundaries into the lakes. These mighty rivers include the Hudson and Mohawk Rivers in New York, the Ohio River, Detroit River, the Saint Louis, and the long and winding Mississippi. There are five Great Lakes in total. They are named Lake Erie, Lake Huron, Lake Michigan, Lake Ontario, and Lake Superior. Lake Superior is the largest freshwater lake in America. These lakes bring in colder air currents than those in states that lie further south due to their northern exposure, so the temperature may drop down to a frigid -20 degrees Fahrenheit. Rainfall and the water that surrounds these states heavily influence the habitats of flora and fauna prevalent in that ecosystem. The shorelines at the edge of the lakes are as sandy as the seashores of the Atlantic and Pacific Oceans, and the Gulf of Mexico. As a consequence, only certain wild berries will flourish there. A

photo by Karen Szklany Gault

few miles further inland, the soil maintains a high level of moisture, and supports tree fruits, nuts, and berries that rely on moist soil to derive their nutrients for flowering and production. They are also fed well by the fallen, decomposing leaves from surrounding plants. The most prolific plants around the Great Lakes are the hardiest varieties of apples, cherries, peaches, pears, apricots, and plums that are best adapted to the cooler temperatures. Rhubarb is also a staple of these states. Hazelnuts, walnuts, pine nuts, hickories, almonds, pecans, and chestnuts can also be found there. Berries that grow best along the lakes and in the nearby forests are brambles, currants, gooseberries, bunch grapes, highbush blueberries, and the hardy kiwifruit. The habitats that will not support fruit, nut, or berry plants are the bogs and swamplands. There is too much standing water in those places, which drowns the roots of fruit trees and plants. The fauna that populate the Great Lakes states are mostly migratory waterfowl, such as geese, ducks, swans, loons, herons, terns, eagles, osprey, kingfishers, and sandpipers that feed on the fruit when they are not catching fish.

New England

Maine, New Hampshire, Vermont, Massachusetts, Rhode Island, and Connecticut are considered the New England states. New York is also included in this classification because the climate of the state most closely matches that of the others listed here. The weather conditions for growing fruits and berries also overlaps closely with that of the Great Lakes region. They may see the same low -20 to -50 degrees Fahrenheit temperatures in the winter. In the summer the climate is sunny, hot, and humid; the temperature reaches a high of 100 degrees Fahrenheit in July and August. The terrain of these states includes mountains, forests, lakes, plains, and the northern Atlantic Ocean. The seashore is often built of high, rocky cliffs. The sandy beaches do not usually support the growth of fruits, nuts, and

berries, unless you grow them in containers or a greenhouse. The mountains, forests, and plains are the friendliest to the hardy fruits, nuts, and berries that often grow in these states. Tree fruits that grow best in New England include apples, pears, hardy peaches, hardy apricots, and European plums. Rhubarb will also grow well on New England soil. Nuts that will grow in this region are hazelnuts (filbert), butternuts, pine nuts, beechnuts, and chestnuts. Berries that produce an abundant yield in these states are strawberries, brambles, highbush blueberries, lingonberries, bunch grapes, and the hardy kiwifruit. Squirrels and chipmunks, nibbling on nuts, are the rodents that symbolize this region in the autumn, as the foliage begins to turn vibrant colors and guests begin to arrive for a slice of apple pie and a cup of warm cider. Falcons, geese, ducks, owls, bats, crows, blue jays, cardinals, and sparrows also feed on the fruits. Bears can be found in the mountains indulging in the berries there, as can the deer, and the moose and caribou of Maine.

For further information about what will grow in your region, please visit the US National Arboretum website at **www.usna.usda.gov/Hardzone/ hrdzon3.html**, which provides a United States Department of Agriculture (USDA) plant hardiness zone map. This map is a picture of the temperature ranges that are experienced in particular regions of the United States, including information that has been cited in this chapter. Many agricultural and gardening sites that you might visit will refer to these zones. That map, including its key to the temperature ranges associated with each zone, will be a useful resource to you throughout the course of your continued gardening adventures.

Now it is time for you to plan your own garden. In the next chapter, your most important task will be walking through the landscape features of your own plot of land.

photo by Martin Miller

CHAPTER 2

· · · · · · · · · · · · ·

What Types of Fruits and Berries Should I Grow?

The possibilities that exist for your own fresh fruit garden are leaping before you. You may be starting to develop a solid idea about which types of fruits and berries you would like to grow. One thing to consider, particularly if you are new to gardening, is which plants will make it into your first season of planting, and which will wait until next year. This decision will depend on the energy you will have to care for your plants throughout their first growing season. You will need to wait a year or two for some of them to flower and produce fruit if you want to plant and grow trees. It may be a good idea to begin with a few different fruits and then add more from year to year. Your back might thank you for this discretion. Keep in mind that diversity is important, so you would want to pick a few varieties of several different types of fruits or berries to grow. The friendly neighborhood honeybees at a colony near you will be very happy about that, which will benefit your long-term gardening plans. With those preliminary details in mind, you are ready to open your door and take a walk through your garden to determine how much space you have, which will determine how many plants you have room to grow. This is a good exercise to complete during the time of day when your garden receives the most direct sunlight.

Grab your sun hat, notebook, pencil, and a tape measure and take a tour around your garden. Begin by noting where the sun is strongest and shines the longest on your land. That is the best spot to concentrate on planting your fruits and berries, because the sun is necessary for feeding the plants and giving them the strength to push forth shoots for flowering and fruit development. You will need the tape measure to determine the length of the rows that reach from one end of your garden space to the other. You will also want to measure the width of your garden. Both pieces of information will be helpful for calculating how many rows of fruit cultivars you will be able to fit in that space.

The final number you will need to use for comparing the amount of space you have to the room you need to plant your fruits and berries is the distance between individual fruit cultivars that is required. Trees will need more breadth around them than brambles and berry bushes because they tend to grow out a wider canopy than the bushes, which can be planted closer together. It might be wise to plant trees that are expected to grow both in volume and height a safe distance from your home, and any other buildings on or near your property. This will guard against any trees crashing through your windows or breaking antennae on your roof in the event of a really bad storm. This method also protects your home from invasion by wild animals, such as raccoons and skunks. An average of 6 to 8 feet is the recommended distance around citrus trees. Citrus trees need a great deal of moisture in the soil that surrounds them, which could damage the foundation of your house. The table below contains the information you need to know about each tree, bramble, bush, and vine so that you will have an idea about how many you will be able to fit in your garden. If the number is the same in both distance columns, the general idea is that this is the amount of space needed on all sides of the tree or plant.

Space Required Between Tree Fruits and Berries

Fruit Species	Space between plants within a Row	Space between Rows
Citrus trees: oranges, mandarins, lemons, limes, grapefruits	12-18 ft.	12-18 ft.
Apricots	20 ft.	20 ft.
Plums	20 ft.	20 ft.
Peaches & Nectarines	15 ft.	15 ft.
Sweet Cherries	20 ft.	20 ft.
Tart Cherries	15-20 ft.	15-20 ft.
Raspberries (brambles)	2-3 ft.	6-12 ft.
Blackberries (brambles)	2-4 ft.	10-12 ft.
Highbush Blueberries	4-5 ft.	8-12 ft.
Halfhigh Blueberries	2 ½ -3 ft.	8-12 ft.
Lowbush Blueberries	1 ft.	8-12 ft.
Rabbiteye blueberries	8 ft.	8-12 ft.
Red & White Currants	3-5 ft.	3-5 ft.
Black Currants	5 ft.	5 ft.
Gooseberries	2-5 ft.	2-5 ft.
Jostaberries	6 ft.	8-12 ft.
Lingonberries	15 in.	15 in.
Strawberries (runners)*	18-24 in.	3-4 in.
Alpine Strawberries (no runners develop)	1 ft.	2 ½ ft.
Kiwifruit – Nonvigorous Vigorous**	8-10 ft. 15-20 ft.	15 ft. 15 ft.
Pineapples	10-12 in.	5 ½ - 6ft.
Melons	3-4 ft.	3-4 ft.
Grapevines	3-5 ft.	Varies with trellis design

*Runners are the offshoots that a "parent" plant is expected to create, from which future cultivars are taken, and from which future fruit crops are expected to grow.
**Vigorous plants produce a high volume crop. Non-vigorous plants produce less.
Data compiled from various sources listed at the end of the book, under Further Reading.

THINGS TO CONSIDER

Within a prevailing regional climate there are microclimates, which are variations of weather contained in a smaller area of land. These are determined partly by the landscape. For example, patches of flat and bare land, will be windier than those that have a grove of pine, oak, or maple. These microclimates can vary from neighborhood to neighborhood, or from city to city. The following list of considerations is provided for you to compare against the landscape features present in your own garden so that you may determine the best pattern for planting your fruits and berries, depending on the sunshine, moisture, and other resources necessary for their growth and productivity.

Topography — lay of the land and soil erosion

The first inventory to record in your notebook is the topography of your land. It may be helpful to draw a rough sketch of your garden to illustrate for yourself what is there. Later you can write-in which fruits you plan to plant in each area. Examples of features to include are: hills, valleys, meadows, lakes, rivers, swamps, seashores, flatlands, deserts, and woodlands. The soil texture and quality is different for each of these features and, therefore, supports different types of plants. For example, if there is an area that is sandy and you would like to grow grapes, this might be the best place to plant a variety that requires a drier soil, such as sea grapes or muscadines. If you have a source of water, such as a lake or stream, you may want to plant blueberries or blackberries close by, because they require dark, moist soil to flower and produce fruit. The more you are able to take advantage of natural features such as these, the less work you will have to do when it is time to begin preparing the land for planting. You will be able to concentrate your efforts toward soil enhancement for the areas that need it most.

Soil quality

As you have noticed, your concern for the amount of nutrients in the soil is dependent upon your local topography. If the land in your backyard is level, the richness of nutrients in the soil is likely to be uniform. If there are various levels of soil on your land, the soil quality may be uneven and each section of your backyard might support a different type of fruit plant. Hills that do not have any tree growth around them are likely to be windier and

the soil on them will be drier. Because of the chill that accompanies the wind, hardier fruit varieties will grow better there.

You will want to have your soil tested for the general level of nutrients present, as well as

photo by Ken Porter

the pH level of your soil, which is whether it is acidic, neutral, or alkaline. Drier, sandier soils located close to house foundations or seashores are usually more alkaline and friendlier to fruits that grow well in those places, such as sea grapes. Dark, moist soils, usually located close to a natural water source or woodland, are more acidic, so they are better places for planting tree fruits and brambles. If your soil is weak in nutrients, you may want to consider preparing your land the autumn prior to the spring you intend to begin planting. If your land is rocky, you may want to collect all the rocks and build a wall at the bottom of a hill so that the soil from the hill does not become eroded. There are seeds to sow for a winter crop cover, particularly over a plateau, and over the seed a layer of organic material would be spread to enrich the quality of the soil and to invite worms to make their own contributions underground. The excrements produced by the worms are referred to as "castings," which function as a potent organic fertilizer for all types of plants. In addition to worms, a variety of insects and microscopic organisms also live underground, in the nutrient-rich soil that you would prepare for planting your fruits and berries. They also feed on the compost that feeds your plants. The fruits you choose to grow will determine the materials you will use to enrich your soil. *For more information about soil enhancement and organic gardening, see Chapter 3.*

Moisture

Regions that have heavy rainfall will support fruit varieties that respond well to this level of moisture. The most important feature of your land is

whether it is prone to standing water. Water needs to drain well for it to be beneficial to your plants. Soil that absorbs the water and feeds the roots of your plants has the capacity to support their growth and survival,

photo by Martin Miller

but standing water, on the other hand, makes the land prone to the development of diseases. One possible solution to this problem would be to dig down deep enough to lay down perforated piping that re-routes the water from areas where it accumulates and spreads it around more evenly. For example, the pipes might carry the water to the periphery of your garden, where the roots of your plants will not have as many competitors for space. This factor is also dependent upon how much sunlight your land receives — the sun causes moisture to evaporate. As a result, trees and plants with greater sunlight will require more manual irrigation with cans, hoses, or sprinklers. Planting a garden near a large body of water, such as a lake, ocean, or river may mean that the air temperature stays warmer than in places farther away from such natural resources. This is primarily because the air currents traveling inland off the water are warmed by the water itself, which absorbs and stores the heat of the sun during the day. The fact that trees often surround these features provides a natural buffer against the inland wind. Regions with hard water that is run through the taps may reduce the acidity of the soil if this water is used for irrigation. For fruit that thrives better in more acidic soils, rainwater collected in a bucket or barrel and used for watering with a can will be more productive.

Climate that supports certain fruits and berries

Warmer climates provide the conditions for growth of fruit trees and berry plants that thrive best in moderate to mild weather patterns. Citrus fruits grow best in the southern states, such as Florida, Eastern Texas, Southern California, Louisiana, Mississippi, and Hawaii. In the colder Northern Pacific, Great Lakes, and Northeastern states, blueberries, blackberries,

 strawberries, and grapes grow more abundantly. The climate of those states supports hardier varieties of tree fruits and berries that can withstand longer periods of dormancy amid winter frost. If you live in one of the Southwest, Mountain, or Midwestern states, or in Northern Alaska, where the wind and nutrient-poor soil limit the types of fruits or berries you can plant directly in the ground, container gardening allows a wider range of options for the fruit species you can grow successfully, and gives you more control over their locations. Containers of a wide variety of materials and sizes can be

used, but they need to be big enough to allow sufficient root growth and to support a heavy, fruit-laden tree. It can be easier to protect plants grown in containers from damaging winds or severe heat because you can move them to a spot with more protective shelter until it is safe to set them outside again. *A section with more detailed information about container growing is included in Chapter 7.* Melons, kiwifruit, avocados, and other fruits that are more acclimated to milder climates may thrive in cooler temperature ranges if a protective layer of polyethylene plastic is laid over a frame built around them during the colder months, particularly if your land lies in a "frost pocket" that poses a risk to freshly planted seedlings. Frost pockets are a result of cold air collected at lower levels of land as the temperatures decrease in the beginning of the colder months of the year. They may also occur during sudden cold spells that occasionally descend after the first warm days of spring. The plastic insulates the seedlings by capturing the heat from the sunlight to warm both the plants and the ground that supports them, almost like a miniature greenhouse. Dwarf varieties of citrus trees, such as limes or kumquats, may produce delicious fruit when carefully tended. Windowsills can be handy for this purpose. You may also want to consider building a greenhouse if you want to raise more tropical fruits than you have window space for, and have enough extra square-footage on your property.

Sunlight and shade — what is available for growing

The importance of sunlight deserves more time. Sunlight is vital to the process of photosynthesis and promotes the cycle of life within each plant. During photosynthesis, light energy from the sun is converted into food for your plants, which gives them the energy they need to flower and grow fruit. The sum of this equation is that the more sunlight available to a plant, the more fruit it will produce. The plant needs the sunlight for the energy and nutrients necessary to produce the fruit you love to eat. This means that the sunniest spots in your garden belong to your fruit trees and berry plants. Leave your shady patches for plants or flowers that are not meant to produce edible fruit. You will be rewarded with a sweet harvest in

the months ahead. Some fruit plants have flowered and produced fruit in more shady areas, but their harvest is typically not as abundant as those given large, daily doses of direct sunlight. There are early and late fruiting varieties that thrive better in different locations. If you have a hilly landscape, you may want to consider this detail. Those that bloom and produce fruit earlier in the year may be planted on a hill facing east to optimize the amount of sunlight available to them. Those that mature later in the year may be planted facing west.

Pollination opportunities for growth and fruiting success

Once an ample supply of sunlight has been guaranteed for your fruits, pollination is your next priority. Honeybees are your most important allies in this endeavor, because they are most responsible for the successful pollination of the flowers that will lead to fruit production. They carry the pollen produced by one flower to flowers on another plant of the same species. The flower that receives the pollen produces the seeds that create more flowers and fruit. The fruit cannot form without the transfer of pollen, so the bees provide an indispensable service to both the plants and the gardeners who faithfully tend to them. In addition to an abundant harvest of fruits and berries, bees produce honey, which benefits the human population through its sweetness, and a measure of relief from a variety of ailments.

Other types of winged, feathered friends that live near your home may also have a vital role in cross-pollinating plants, just by eating them and roaming around your property. Hummingbirds have long beaks that they

use to drink nectar from flowers. Pollen from the flowers settles on the bird's beak, thus traveling aboard its mouth to where it needs to go. Some of the plant varieties available, such as some blueberry varieties, have been developed by agriculturalists at commercial nurseries to be self-pollinating, a process by which the wind does most of the work. Even those types of fruit plants are more productive when placed next to another plant of the same species. Other species that depend on the bees and birds include varieties that are strong pollen-*producers* (male), which must be planted in close proximity to the varieties that bear flowers with the vital pollen-*receiving* anatomy (female) in order to bear fruit. If the "male" pollen-producing variety is not planted near the "female" pollen-receiving variety, very few flowers will grow, and these plants will not produce fruit. If they are, both will bear an abundant crop of healthy fruit. Examples of such fruit species are cherries, plums, apricots, kiwis, some blueberries, Asian pears, and muscadine grapes.

It takes time to be able to identify these varieties, so a trusted nursery staff member who is familiar with the fruit species you are interested in will be able to guide you toward the selections that will work best for you. *The reproductive anatomy of flowers is discussed in greater detail in Chapter 5 of this book.*

Available space — how much of each fruit can be planted

The amount of your favorite fruits that you will grow depends on how much space you have in your garden. The measurements you took note of earlier have now become important. If you plan to place some of your trees at the edges of your property, you may wish to consult with your neighbors, some of whom may be willing to have a section of their lawn strewn with fallen ripe fruit or berries in exchange for a share in the harvest. If making decisions about what to plant this year and what must wait for another year is causing some trouble, you might be able to grow a few of your chosen fruits in containers. Some fruits, such as strawberries, are easily grown in pots or tubs that can be used to adorn a patio or balcony. Some dwarf lemons, limes, or mandarin oranges would also add an extra splash of color and zest to your patio décor. A can may be used to water these plants, so your options are increased if your water source is too far away to reach certain areas of your yard, even with a long hose or a sprinkler. You would also have a shorter walk from your kitchen to your fruit when you want to make a quick salad. This will enable you to leave some of the ground space in your garden for other fruits that need more room to grow. *The steps for growing fruits and berries in movable containers are described in greater detail in Chapter 7.*

There are some fruits that take less space to grow and allow you to add beautiful features that hold something edible to your garden. Vine fruits can be trained to climb fences and walls to save space, while they beautify and offer extra privacy where it is desired. Berry bushes can be planted as natural barriers between your home and the pedestrian traffic just beyond your property. They also provide vibrant color to your yard in spring and autumn. In addition to more privacy, a fruit tree would provide extra shade to keep you cool during the hot summer months when it is full-grown.

Disease and insect resistance — the survival of fruits and berries

There are some fruit and berry plants that have been cultivated for resistance against pests and diseases. It is important to find out which pests and diseases have attacked certain fruits and berries planted by close neighbors. This will give you the information you need to purchase a cultivar grown for resistance to such threats. You might want to choose fruit and berry plants that are healthy enough to put up a strong resistance to the challenges your garden soil may present. Many times, fruit trees of one fruit species, such as an orange tree, are grafted onto the root system of one that is more resistant to diseases. Plant nursery staff members, who cultivate such fruits professionally, will be able to tell you how it was done and how well the cultivar they have created will stand up to potential disease threats. They will also be able to point out where the graft union is located on a particular plant, and to inform you about what you can do to protect your fruit plants from pests and diseases during both the planting process and while providing ongoing care. For example, they may let you know that in order to reduce the risk of your fruit plant becoming vulnerable to a fungal disease, it is best not to plant it in soil where roses, potatoes, tomatoes, eggplant, or peppers have recently grown. It is also best to leave room between the roots of the tree and organic compost that is added to the soil when planting a tree, bramble, bush, or vine. In addition to the above precautions, planting varieties that are particularly resistant to pests and diseases will make less work for you in the long run.

Underground structural obstacles

Make sure there are no wells, underground power sources, or pipes for water, gas, or sewage. The roots of trees could interfere with or damage their functioning. This would also interfere with the long-term health and productivity of your tree or plant, because a source of underground wiring could become entangled in tree roots and suffocate the tree. An underground well would pose a barrier that would stop the further growth of tree roots. If the roots wrap around pipes, those pipes could burst and poison the tree, if not the entire garden. A gas explosion would be dangerous for both humans and plants, as would a fire from a short in underground electrical circuits.

BEST SEASONS

You have finished the tour of your garden and are now empowered with pages of notes and a diagram of where you want to plant your favorite fruits and berries. The next concern that arises in the planting process is about the timing of your planting. The table below indicates in which season each type of fruit is best planted, and when the fruit on the tree is generally ripe enough to be harvested. This information is vital to the process of planning your garden, including the timing of placing an order with a nursery for particular plants and seeds. The chart pertains to the most common varieties of the fruit species listed. Other varieties of the same fruits may bloom earlier or later.

Planting and Harvesting Seasons for Fruits and Berries

Name of Fruit or Berry	Planting Season	Harvesting Season
Apple tree	Early Spring	Late July into Late Fall
Apricot tree	Early Spring	July or August
Blackberry bush	Early Spring	June or July
Blueberry shrub (ornamental)	Spring in most of US; fall in the South	Midsummer
Cantaloupe vine	Two weeks after last frost	Midsummer
Cherry tree	Spring	June and July
Elderberry shrub	Spring (North) or Fall (South)	August and September
Gooseberry and Currant shrubs	Spring or Fall	Late Spring through Summer
Grape vine	Late Spring	October
Kiwi vine	Spring	Late summer
Lingonberry shrub	Spring, after danger of frost	July
Mulberry tree	Spring	Early Summer to Midsummer
Peach, Nectarine, and Almond trees	Spring	August
Pear tree	Spring	August for early varieties
Plum tree	Spring	August for early varieties
Raspberry cane	Spring; transplant Early Spring	July
Rhubarb plant	Early Spring (North); Fall (South)	Late Spring; All Summer
Strawberry plant	Early Spring (N. Hemisphere); Late Fall (S. Hemisphere)	June, through Fall
Watermelon vine	Spring (after danger of frost)	Late June, early July
Kiwifruit – Nonvigorous Vigorous	8-10 ft. 15-20 ft.	15 ft. 15 ft.
Pineapples	10-12 in.	5 ½-6 ft.
Melons	3-4 ft.	3-4 ft.
Grapevines	3-5 ft.	Varies with trellis design

*Data compiled from various sources listed at the end of the book, under *Further Reading*.

Planting seasons

As indicated in the table above, spring is the optimal time to plant fruit trees and berry plants in the northern regions of the country. But in the South, the opposite is true. The importance of this timing has much to do with the establishment of root systems for the plants before the extremes of temperature set in. In the North, gardeners wait for the dire cold of winter to be behind them before planting their fruit. In the South, the summer climate is too hot and humid for fruit plants to survive, so the best planting season is autumn. The timing of fertilizer application and sowing the cover crop also depends on this difference. It is important to avoid applying any fertilizing agents to the ground around your trees and plants immediately before they enter dormancy if you live in a region that experiences a colder climate in the winter. A better time to apply fertilizer is in spring, shortly before they are expected to produce buds and blossom.

Harvesting

Each species of fruit becomes ripe in its own time. Some have specific months in which they normally ripen, and either fall off the tree or are picked by hand, such as apricots that ripen in August, and grapes that are ripe in October. Others are less regular and will require attention to the attributes that correspond to ripeness in that particular fruit rather than reliance on a par-

ticular month for optimal harvesting. Fruits that fall into this category include apples, gooseberries, currants, mulberries, melons, and kiwis. Different varieties of one fruit may be harvested at different times of the year. Some may be early bloomers while the fruit of others ripens later, such as the June-bearing strawberry that ripens at the beginning of the summer, and the day-neutral variety that ripens over the course of the entire summer. *At the end of the book, Appendix A lists Internet resources that provide information on the growth habits of specific varieties, which may also include when to expect your first harvest.* For some fruit trees, you may need to nurture their growth for several years before you reap the benefits of your labors.

CASE STUDY: PLANTING, GROWING, AND HARVESTING CITRUS TREE FRUITS IN FLORIDA

Bill Murphy is a veteran home gardener who lives in Beverly Hills, Florida. He has been growing citrus trees for five years. The climate in Florida is temperate; it is a state in which there is seldom snow or long periods of freezing temperatures. Though the climate is friendliest to citrus trees, there have been several incidences of early frost that could threaten them if they are left unprotected.

"When the trees were young, I created a teepee with 11 ft. x 16 ft. tarps and 10 ft. PVC poles, using a ladder to climb up and lay the tarp over the tree and the poles," he said.

As the trees grew bigger, this could not be done, Murphy said. So, he used well water in sprinklers, temperature-controlled at 70 degrees Fahrenheit. "Coating the trunk and heavy branches with ice can also protect them from freezing damage," he said.

The lot where Murphy planted his trees is one acre — 200 ft. wide and 250 ft. deep. The front faces south and the back faces north. The trees are located in a line facing east to west. They stand 15 feet in front of a growth of pine and oak trees, which protects them from wind damage and allows for good sunshine for most of the day. The process he used for preparing the ground for planting his citrus trees involved removing roots from other trees and plants from the ground. The soil was sandy, so he added 5 gallons of peat moss to each planting hole to improve the quality. Most of the peat he placed at the bottom of the holes, but he also placed some over the top after the holes were re-filled, at the base of the young trees. Once planted, he gave them an inch of water each week.

Murphy planted his trees between the months of May and August. Their growing season lasts from March through November. Presently, the trees are 14 feet high and may still grow taller. They begin to flower in February. If there are periods of frost after that, they may re-flower each time, with or without forming fruit. He has seen a tree re-blossom three times in one year. The lemon trees yield an average of 75 lemons per tree and the Ruby Red grapefruit trees yield an average of 35 grapefruits per tree. Periods of unseasonably cold temperatures affect the amount of yield that the trees produce, rather than the timing. They are usually ripe for harvesting in December, though some of them may be ripe enough to eat by Thanksgiving.

SOME FINAL NOTES ABOUT PERSONAL PREFERENCE

Along with some of the practical considerations that come with planning a garden of edible fruit, there are things that you will want to include in your garden because you find pleasure in them. They are the things that will make your garden more inviting to you, and will express your pride in the space you have created. The following suggestions may help you use your unique style preferences to your best advantage, by ensuring that they serve more than one purpose.

If you live in a city where there is more wall or fence space than yard on your property, you might like to use that wall as a source of beauty by growing plants against it. You might even want to erect a trellis, which is a frame made of poles and wire on which you would train a grape vine or raspberry runners to climb, wrap around, and grow from. There are different designs and methods for training your trees or plants to grow in a certain pattern on a particular surface. Grapes grow well on trellises and on pergolas, which are wooden frames with a latticework roof that supports the growth of grape vines. They can serve as a shady bower under which you may want to sit and read a book on sunny mornings and afternoons. The blackberry bush is a climbing plant that will also grow well against a wall or around a fence. Roger Swain, a former host of the PBS *Victory Gardens* series, recommends Chester blackberries as the hardiest thorn-less variety for this purpose. Apple and pear trees can also be trained successfully to grow that way, as can berries, including currants, gooseberries, blackberries, and raspberries.

Finally, as a compromise between container gardening and planting your fruits and berries directly into the ground, raised beds may be an attractive option. They are boxes that are made of wood or plastic, into which you place soil for planting. If your soil is weak in nutrients and needs to be prepared before it will be able to support growing fruit, you may still be able to use the land that you have planned for garden cultivation to grow your fruit in raised beds. You would need to build or purchase a bed, into which you would place nutrient-rich soil. This soil could be homemade from a mixture of worm castings, organic compost, and mulch materials, or it may be purchased from a nursery or a farm. The bed would need to be deep enough to plant a melon vine, berry bush, bramble, or grape vine cultivar, and allow room for the roots to grow. Brambles that have thorny branches are generally hardier than those that do not, and would be more likely to survive being transplanted into a raised bed. These are the fruits that may be best trained on trellises or other garden features for extra support. Another advantage of raised beds is that you should not have to bend down as far as you would have to when planting directly into the soil, which will be nicer to your back when it is time to attend to their ongoing care.

With your notebook filled with garden measurements and a rough sketch that illustrates your intended layout, it is time to take the next step toward planting your fruit garden. Before purchasing seeds or cultivars to plant, it is important to prepare the soil so that it will support the fruit you are eager to grow. *Chapter 3 provides the details that will lead you to create the best soil for growing the most delicious fruits and berries.*

CHAPTER 3

. . . . ◆

Soil Texture, Quality, and Enrichment

T his is your chance feel like a kid by getting back into the sandbox and getting your hands dirty. You may even have a chance to make a mud pie or two. Just keep the grass out of them. The dirt is where the action is, for now. You will feed your plants from that level so that they will feed you later. It is time to don your most comfortable clothes and a pair of sturdy boots, roll up your sleeves, grab a spade, and start digging.

If you have not yet sent a sample of your soil to a lab for testing, this is the time to do it. Details for this procedure are provided below, in the next section. If the land in your garden varies in elevation, you may want to have the soil at each level tested. The quality of soil may vary from one level to another. You need to know how many vitamins are milling around down under your dirt, as well as the presence of other microscopic organisms that may be crawling around down there. Your soil test results will also

photo by Ken Porter

give you information about other qualities present in the soil, such as its pH level, which will be described further in the next section. It is important to make sure the soil is tested for its pH level, in addition to having it tested for potassium, calcium, magnesium, iron, zinc, and other nutrients. Each fruit and berry plant has its own preference for the amount of pH in the soil where it grows.

Testing for the presence of heavy metals and other toxins is also very important, because it will yield useful information about whether or not your garden soil is safe for growing food. The level of lead present is one of the most important factors, particularly if you will be feeding young children. Toxins do not break down, so planting in raised beds may be necessary if such tests are returned to you with results that indicate their presence.

SOIL TESTING

You will want to send a soil sample to a laboratory for testing. It is important to follow the directions they give you for preparing the sample, including where to send it. You may call and order one from your local state university. State university systems usually have extensions where students may gain additional certification and experience in a specialized field, such as agriculture or chemistry. For example, in New England the University of Massachusetts Extension on its Amherst campus is a frequent resource for soil testing. They have published a brochure that gives directions for preparing a test sample to send to their laboratory, which may be found online at **www.umass.edu/soiltest**.

To gather your test sample, follow these steps:

1. Gather your tools — you will need a spade, trowel, and plastic or glass container (such as a freezer bag that holds a gallon of food).

2.   Clear away grass and plant debris from the top of the soil.

3.   Dig into the soil with the spade and remove a section of soil that is about 6 inches deep and 6 inches wide. Using the trowel, dig out a small scoop of soil from the bottom of the hole and place it in the container.

4.   Mix together a composite of soil from 12 different spots in your garden for each sample.

5.   Gather together all of the information the lab requested and then send it in along with the sample. If you plan to keep an organic garden, request that the lab include organic amendment recommendations.

There are several sources for ordering your own soil testing kit. One online resource is named LaMotte's. Their URL is **www.biconet.com/ testing/LaMGarden.html**. A variety of soil testing kits that include different combinations of testing chemicals are available for purchase from that site. If you purchase one of those do-it-yourself soil-testing kits, the cost ranges from $17.50 to $64, with the more expensive testing kits including more supplies.

There are different qualities to have your soil tested for. The basic test results reflect the nutrients present in your soil that will feed the growth of your fruit trees and berry plants. The elements that you will want your soil tested for are nitrogen, phosphorus, potassium, and the pH level of the soil. If the soil you will be growing your fruits and berries in has had trouble supporting plant growth in the past, you may want to have the soil tested for micronutrients and nematodes. Nematodes are worm-like parasites that feed on tree roots. They are the cause of many diseases developed by berry bushes. These are all things that may be lurking unseen in the deep dark soil under the ground and you will want to have some control over their effect on the fruits and berries you will be growing. *Examples of pests such as these and the havoc they cause will be discussed in greater detail in Chapter 8.*

Not all tests will pick up specific viruses that may exist in your soil. The symptoms of such diseases may be visible only on the leaves of plants, such as red ring spots on highbush blueberries, or through fruit forming on the stem and dropping on the ground before they are ripe. Sometimes, the virus may run its course and the plants will recover enough to return a better yield the following season. However, the disease can spread. Examples of such blights are the blueberry red ringspot virus and the strawberry mottle virus, which have been spread more broadly in the Pacific Northwest states. To prevent the development and spread of diseases, it is important to buy your seedlings from a nursery that is a producer of cultivars certified as free of disease.

ACID VS. ALKALINE

Use the following table to help you understand the breakdown of what the pH levels mean for gardeners who are interested in growing fruits and berries. It is the measure of the active hydrogen (H) concentration in the soil. This test reveals its level of acidity. The number assigned to your soil will be between 1 and 14. If the numeric result you receive is close to 7, your soil is considered neutral and generally good for growing fruit. The pH range associated with neutrality is between 6.0 and 7.0.

If the result is a pH less than 6.0, the soil is considered too acidic, meaning that it may have too much moisture and may drown the roots or render them vulnerable to fungal and other types of diseases instead of assisting their establishment. This could be caused by low amounts of lime or the application of too much fertilizer. In order to raise the pH, you would need to add lime to neutralize the pH level. Lime is made of ground limestone, dolomite, or calcified seaweed. Wood ashes are another good additive. Blueberry and lingonberry plants thrive better in moister, acidic soil with a pH between 4.5 and 5.5. The states of the Pacific Northwest and New England are the best places to grow those berries.

If the pH is above 7.0 it is considered alkaline, which means that it contains too little moisture. This type of soil is found in dry, arid climates, such as deserts. You would need to add manure, peat moss, cottonseed meal, composted oak leaves, and a mulch of pine needles to neutralize it. Sulfur may also be used to neutralize alkaline soils, but using this method has been reported to ruin the taste of some fruit, such as rendering a metallic taste in grapes and the wine that is made from them. The process also causes loss of some nutrients, such as Vitamin C. Most grape vines will thrive in soil with a range of 6.0 to 7.5 pH, with the muscadine variety the most amenable to greater alkalinity. Southern California and the Southeastern states are great places to grow those types of grapes.

As you become a knowledgeable gardener, you will be able to read more about what your soil is telling you. You will be able to determine the types of fruits and berries that will grow best in it. You now know that the pH level is closely related to the amount of moisture the ground will soak up or drain out, and how much of the mushy decomposed kitchen scraps or dried leaves from last autumn you will need to feed the roots when you begin planting. In the meantime, dig a hole and grab a handful of the dirt in your garden. How does it feel? Is it soft and dry, dark and moist, or hard and caked together? Is it light brown, dark brown, or red? If it is light brown, soft, and dry, the soil is sandy, very alkaline, and will not retain much water. If it is dark and moist, it retains water and is likely to be more acidic. Soil that is hard and caked together is known as clay, usually appears red, and will need to be mixed with the darker moist soil in order to support the growth of fruits and berries. A description of the different types of soil you may encounter and how they affect the production of fruit is provided in the next section.

Level of pH Required for Growing a Variety of Fruits and Berries

Fruit or Berry Variety	Soil pH Requirement	Quality (Acidic or Alkaline)
Blackberry	5.5-7.0	Alkaline
Grape	6.0-7.5	Alkaline
Strawberry	6.5-6.8	Neutral
Raspberry	6.0-6.8	Neutral
Currant	6.2-6.5	Neutral
Gooseberry	6.2-6.5	Neutral
Citrus: grapefruits, oranges, lemons, limes	5.0-5.5	Acidic
Rhubarb	5.5-6.5	Acidic
Kiwifruit	5.0-6.5	Acidic
Lingonberry	4.5-5.5	Acidic
Blueberry	4.5-5.5	Acidic

TYPES OF SOIL

The texture of the soil in your garden is very important to you because it indicates what you will need to do to help your garden flourish. All soils have the potential to grow a diverse collection of plants if they are worked with effectively. Some take more work to get them where you want them than others do. Sand is the most porous; which means that it contains too many holes for water to escape through, so that the water is not held long enough to fully irrigate roots properly. It is dry and is good to have as a resource for plants that need to grow in soil that is more alkaline. Sand supports the American pawpaw fruit, which was depended upon by Native Americans hundreds of years ago. The taste of the pawpaw has been compared to both the mango and the banana, and was referred to as the "poor man's banana" when it grew more abundantly across the country. It is now rarely grown. One advantage of growing fruits that prefer more alkaline soil for growth and crop production is that they are maintained more easily in times of drought.

If you have other types of fruit in mind, sandy soil may need to be amended, or added to, in order to support a more diverse collection of plant life. The amendments that can be added include food scraps (not meat or dairy), dead flowers, fallen leaves, fallen bark from trees, worm castings, loamy soil, and hay. Adding a layer of hay on your garden soil would keep in the warmth and moisture generated by the application of organic materials.

On the other hand, a soil that is already dark and loamy does not need much amendment if you are interested in growing citrus and other types of tropical fruits. If there is any of it to spare, it can be used to moisten drier, sandier patches of ground. Some soils are mixed together to create a more neutral pH that suits some fruit trees and plants, because they contain a balance of nutrients and moisture. The loam would need to be amended with sand if you want to grow blueberries, strawberries, blackberries, raspberries, currants, and other types of berries that prefer more neutral soil.

One of the most amazing aspects of the natural world is that for every problem that arises in one place, a solution can be found somewhere else. So, if your soil is too sandy, the scraps from your food become part of the earth again and give it moisture, filling your new fruits with extra vitamins. The fallen leaves and branches from trees that may already be part of the natural landscape surrounding your garden are also a fantastic form of organic fertilizer. If the soil is too moist, it can be balanced with an inch or two of sand raked in to make it more amenable to growing fruits. Nature takes care of herself, and also helps you create new life using her materials. Nature also gives you creatures to help with the process of breaking down natural materials to create soil. If there are worms and bugs living in your garden, you are well on your way to sustainable soil with which to create a garden of plenty, produced by healthy fruit trees and berry plants.

Sandy soil

Sandy soil is found close to a home's foundation and consists of particles of finely ground stone with large pore spaces between them. It is subject to

erosion, wind, and rain. Water runs through sandy soil instead of being retained, so it is poor in the nutrients that will feed the growth of healthy plants. If used as it is, you may observe sea grapes or muscadines flourishing in sandy soil. One advantage of sandy soil is that it is light and more easily worked than other soils. Adding a generous amount of compost and mulch will increase its level of fertility. Communities that live in desert ecosystems have been able to grow food on sandy soil by doing just that. If combined with loam, sandy soil will support the growth of a variety of berries, such as blueberries, strawberries, and brambles.

Gravelly Soil

Gravelly soil is made up of tiny stones and is also found close to the foundation of your home. Water is absorbed quickly by this soil, which prevents fruit trees and plants from receiving the moisture they need to thrive. It is heavier than sand and does not hold any nutrients for growing, so the task of amending it is greater, mainly because of its weight. Shrubs that bear ornamental berries usually eaten by birds instead of humans grow well in gravelly soil. Examples of these are buckthorn, hawthorn, holly, and honeysuckle. Instead of trying to raise fruit edible to humans in such a harsh soil environment, creating raised beds filled with organic soil of your own construction or growing fruit in attractive containers made of a variety of materials, such as clay and porcelain, may be better uses of your time and energy. If there is a water table on part of your land, you may be able to transfer the gravel to that area to soak up the water so that it does not stand very long. This will make it more amenable to trees and plants that are susceptible to fungal diseases. Creating a rock garden as a complement to the patches of land where you will be growing trees, bushes, and other fruit plants may be a good use for the more gravelly areas of your garden. The gravel could also be used for creating a walking path through the garden. If you have such material at your disposal, you may have a creative edge for enhancing your garden's beauty and accessibility.

Silty soil

Silt is moist sand with a silky texture. The particles are smaller and have fewer pores between them than sandy soil. It is also a more fertile type of soil because it retains more water. Because it holds water more readily, this soil might also need to be monitored. Water may not drain very quickly, and young fruit plants may be threatened by standing water. As a gardening resource, silt is often used in the same manner as loam, adding moisture to clay or dry sand. The pH is more alkaline than loam, so plants that grow best under those conditions produce fruit if planted in silt, such as gooseberries and currants. These berries also like garden plots that are partially shaded for most of the day. A shady spot on the northern side of the garden with silt as the main soil texture is the ideal environment for those berries.

Clay soil

Clay soil contains very fine, weathered particles with a high capacity to hold water. It is sticky to the touch, can be dense with very little air passing through, and is slow to warm in the spring. This means that the soil may not be warm in time to plant most cultivars of fruits and berries. It certainly would not work for growing citrus trees and other subtropical fruits. Because clay soil retains moisture, the root areas of young plants can become waterlogged and prone to fungal diseases. If left dry for too long, it becomes hard and impenetrable. Adding silt to the clay may add more balance to the moisture levels in the soil. Gardeners faced with clay soil will need to amend it to increase its fertility for growing most fruits and berries. Clay tends to have a high level of alkalinity and needs to be combined with organic compost material to soften it and increase its fertility for raising fruits.

Chalky soil

Chalky soil, like sand and gravel, contains mainly large particles that drain water easily, and has a similar level of alkalinity. A limited range of plants will grow in this type of soil. Providing moisture for fruits and berries planted in this soil will be hard work. Its texture is hard on tools such as spades, too. Such a soil would need to be treated with a nutrient-rich loam and organic compost so that it will retain more water and attract worms. Currant plants that are more tolerant of dry soils may grow successfully as a result of these efforts. Aside from this edible plant, flowering bushes such as holly, forsythia, bamboo, and desert yuccas are better suited to growing in this environment.

Peaty soil

This type of soil is so dark it is almost black, and it is found in swamps and bogs. It retains water to the point of soaking through the winter months, but tends to stay dry in the summer, unless soaked through manually. Its texture is spongy and it is light to turn. It is a boon to have peat in your garden if you discover it there, particularly if the rest of your garden soil is sandy. Peat contains a great amount of organic material, but may need to be amended with compost and mulch in order to offer fruit plants, such as blueberry bushes and citrus trees, enough nutrients and water retention to grow and produce. It will also need frequent watering throughout the growing season.

Loamy Soil

Loam is a mixture of sand, clay, and silt, with medium-sized particles that are gritty and rich in nutrients. It drains water well, but does not become completely dry. Loam is commonly found in woodlands and pastures. Adding manure or compost to loam will enhance its fertility beyond the level it naturally offers on its own, which would be most beneficial to soil that has been left unused for several years. It is often added to drier, more alkaline soils to increase their level of supportive nutrients. In the spring, loam warms up quickly so it is ready as early as March for planting and sowing seeds, which is earlier than clay or silt alone would be. Loam is friendliest to growing small fruits, such as strawberries, currants, mulberries, blackberries, and blueberries.

Mixing different soil types together may help to increase the ability of each type to grow your favorite fruits and berries, but there are also ways that you can help your soil become more fertile. Many people have found that keeping worms in their homes and feeding them their kitchen scraps saves time, energy, and financial resources. Keeping a worm bin is an excellent method for creating organic soil amendments that are rich in nutrients. It is also a great source of bait for those who enjoy fishing.

CREATING ORGANIC SOIL WITH WORMS

When you dug deep into your garden to observe the soil there, you may have seen some signs of life that squirmed, crawled, and scuttled about. These wet, squirmy creatures are a sign of healthy soil. If there are no worms, spiders, beetles, and other bugs in your soil, then there is no point in trying to plant and grow fruit in it. If it will not support one type of life, it is not likely to support another very well. Where there are worms and bugs dancing around underground, the soil is likely to support plant life, particularly plants that produce fruits and berries. Worms eat food scraps and break them down into organic soil. They also eat leaves and other natural debris that fall to the ground. The bugs help to break it down further over time. That is one of the foundations of organic gardening.

Why use worms?

People are going crazy over worms these days. It may seem as if all types of worms are on demand, but only one type is. Red wigglers are the only ones known to break down natural food waste into castings. The castings are the worms' waste material, which fortifies soil with an abundance of nutrients. Earthworms also lighten the soil to prevent water-logging and increase the underground airflow. They also eat up some of the fruit and vegetable waste that would normally need to be composted manually, saving you the time and energy you would otherwise spend bringing the compost out to a bin, covering it with layers of hay, and turning it with a shovel. The process by which worms are used to break down your kitchen scraps is called vermicomposting.

There are many reasons why people have begun to compost natural waste using worms. At the top of the list is the amount of time and energy it saves. There is no need to pay for operating a garbage disposal machine in your sink, so you waste less water and electricity. Less garbage is sent to landfills, so the earth is saved from the pollution caused by garbage truck usage. Worm bins do not attract the pests that would be interested in the contents of garbage cans and produce fewer odors than the garbage can. They also take up very little space and do not require much time to maintain. In return, they give you a free source of soil amendments and live fishing bait. Below is a description of the steps involved in establishing a worm colony in your home.

Where to find the worms

The best earthworms to use for composting are small and red. Their scientific name is *Eisenia foetida*, but they are generally called "red wigglers." If you do not find any worms in your own backyard, you may order them from a worm farm and have them mailed to you. If you visit **www.worms. com/worm-a-roo.html**, you can buy some supplies for keeping worms, including the worms themselves. Some of the worms may arrive in cans — a "Can-O-Worms" costs $110. A "worm factory" costs $93, a "Vermi-hut" costs $79, and a "Worm Chalet" is $189. Gardening magazines that focus on organic practices may contain ads for other places where you can purchase your worms, too. *For more information about Internet resources for purchasing and maintaining earthworms, see Appendix A.* Your local nursery or gardening center may also be able to help you find a reliable source for acquiring red worms.

Where to keep the worms

The container that worms are kept in is called a worm bin, and may be kept in the kitchen, basement, or outside gardening shed. You may create one yourself, or order it from a website such as "Worm-a-Roo." Bins are usually made of wood or plastic, but wood has been reported to keep the worms cooler during the summer months. In addition to the material of the bin and the storage space where it is kept, its size will depend on the amount of food scraps your family produces each week — 1 square foot for every pound of kitchen waste that your household uses each week. Once the kitchen scraps are eaten by the worms, they are turned into castings, which is their waste. Enough room needs to be given for the worms to live as they produce those castings, which will fertilize your soil. For a family of three that produces about 3 ½ pounds of food scraps per week, a box that is 2 feet wide, 2 feet long, and 8 inches deep would be a good size. A 2 ft. x 3 ft. box with the same depth is suitable for four to six people who produce about 6 pounds of waste per week. It must have air holes at the top and drainage holes at the bottom. The water that collects at the bottom of the bin is called worm tea, and it is also nutrient-rich. No matter where you keep your worms, keep in mind that they are happiest in the temperature range of 55 to 77 degrees Fahrenheit.

Furnishing a home for the worms

Within the worm bin, a bed of shredded paper can be laid on slatted boards and placed on sand or gravel for good water drainage. Their bedding is best made of fluffy material, such as shredded paper, which allows the worms to breathe, burrow, and bury their castings. Other sources of bedding are shredded fallen leaves and peat moss from the forest floor. On top of their bedding, place a layer of vegetable waste, covered by wet, non-glossy newspaper. Suitable sources of the compost to feed them include crushed eggshells, coffee grounds, tea bags, coffee filters, grains, and the uneaten remains of fruits and vegetables. It is important to feed them organic kitchen waste that contains no meat or dairy products. Nor should they be fed grass of any type — it is fatal to them. Their favorite foods include cantaloupe, watermelon, and pumpkin.

Care of the worms

Earthworms need to be sprinkled with a handful of water each day in order to remain moist — once a day is sufficient if they are kept cool enough. A

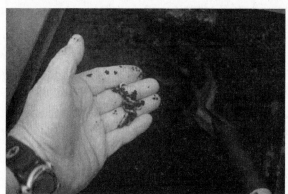

photo by Ken Porter

bin that allows sufficient air and water to flow through it, and houses them in a way that keeps them comfortable, will support the life of your worms and the production of rich, organic soil to feed your fruit plants.

When the bin is full, the worms are separated or sorted out of their castings, and the castings are put into a bucket, so that what they have produced may be spread in your garden to feed your plants. The castings usually do not have an odor and are more like soil than waste. After completing this process, their beds are remade with fresh material and the bin is returned to its usual spot.

CASE STUDY:
A BIN OF WORMS
NAMED "STEVE"

Ken Porter inherited his worms from a class of third grade students who were being taught about the process of vermicomposting as a science lesson. Their teacher demonstrated what could be done with biodegradable kitchen waste, using worms as the means for breaking down that waste. All the worms were named Steve so that each time a worm was pulled out to observe, the students could greet the worm by name, saying, "Hi Steve." The worm bin was kept in the classroom during the school year, but when it moved into his home for summer vacation, Porter began feeding them and has not stopped since.

Porter used the worm castings to improve the soil quality of his houseplants and small gardens at first, because he lived in an apartment in Boston when he began keeping them. He noticed that his plants became greener and flowered more when he fed them with the worm castings, which he used as a fertilizer. He also watered his plants with "worm tea," which is the water that collects at the bottom of the worm bin, beneath the bed.

The red worms that Porter and his spouse bought in the year 2000 were ordered from "Worm-a-Roo," an online red worm and worm care supply vendor. Since then, friends of his have started their own collection from that bunch of worms. When his original collection died, he started a new collection from the offspring of his original worm family. He is not certain what the average life span of one of his worms is, but sees that new young worms are always present in his bins.

"They multiply fast when there is a lot of food," he said. When asked what he feeds to his worms, he said that he gives them "trimmings from vegetables and leftovers from the refrigerator. They will not eat moldy food, but wilted lettuce or spinach is great." If he wants to speed up the process of compost consumption, he drops the scraps into a food blender to puree them. He is careful not to overwhelm the worms with too much compost so that he does not create an unhealthy environment in the bins. Coffee grounds are good food for the worms, but meat and dairy are not. Bread and pasta are okay in small amounts. He sprinkles some finely ground eggshells or fine, clean sand into the compost often, to provide them with the grit they need to "chew things up." He also sprinkles some "worm tea" over the compost to encourage the bacteria in the bin to break down the food matter more quickly.

"I feed the worms twice a week with kitchen scraps and coffee grounds, which we collect in a plastic container. When it is full, it goes down to the worm bin," Porter said. "I make sure that the castings and compost are kept moist, and have a container of water by the bins to make it easy to give them a sprinkle." In Boston, the water was chlorinated, so he left the water to stand for a day or two before using it for the worms. Now that his water comes from a well, he no longer needs to do that. One step that he does take is to use a small hand rake to occasionally turn over the castings, or soil. He said that his worms produce four to six cubic feet of castings per year, which he keeps in an uncovered bucket in his basement for use during spring planting season and beyond. The bucket is left uncovered so that the worms that inevitably end up leaving the bin with the castings are not suffocated. They are also good for the soil that the castings will feed, if they are not found and returned to their original home.

Now that Porter has moved into a townhouse in a co-housing village in Massachusetts, he keeps his worms in their original "Worm-a-Roo" bin in his basement, which is cool. He estimates that the average temperature down there is between 50 and 60 degrees Fahrenheit. He checks on them most often in the summer to make sure that they are cool enough, and his basement seems to be the perfect spot to keep them happy. Steve's worm family seems to have adapted very well to their new home and have produced plenty of castings for Porter to use in his gardens, and some to share with neighbors. Their castings will be used for growing raspberries, blueberries, and other fruit this summer.

FEEDING YOUR SOIL

The subject of composting with worms highlights the importance of feeding your soil so that it is the most fertile for growing your fruits and berries. The worm castings and tea are one form of fertilizer that feeds your soil a multitude of nutrients, naturally. The next section digs deeper into the world of animal poop to dish about the merits in the remains of a variety of feathered and four-legged friends.

You may be wondering what else might exist to feed your soil while you wait for your worms to produce a sufficient supply of castings and tea for an entire garden. There are more options for feeding your garden soil that are also organic, meaning that they are derived from living organisms in the natural world, and that will break back down into the soil over time. These include mulch, compost, and animal manure.

Mulch materials for fertile soil

Mulch materials are natural resources that enhance the quality of your garden soil. They contribute vital nutrients that are needed for growing plants that produce edible food, such as tree fruits, nuts, and berries. When you had your soil tested, some of the nutrients that the laboratory staff looked for included natural elements such as nitrogen, phosphorus, and potassium. Nitrogen supports the growth and deep green color of stems and leaves. Phosphorus stimulates root formation, and strengthens roots that have already developed. Potassium, also called potash, contributes to the development of flowers and fruits, and increases the plants' level of resistance to disease.

Organic mulch materials are accessible at a very low cost, and are used both individually and in combination to feed the soil and increase its fertility.

Adding layers of mulch also protects the soil from temperature extremes, keeping it warmer in the winter, which means that your plants have a greater chance of surviving the colder months. Keeping the soil cooler in the summer, mulch boosts water retention and suppresses weed growth. This saves you time by reducing the amount of watering and weeding you will need to do throughout the growing season. Mulches are often used to customize your soil to the needs of your fruit plants by altering the pH level. A variety of mulch materials are described below according to their composition, properties, and the nutrients they contribute to your garden soil.

Humus

Humus is the darkest, richest form of mulch you can give your soil because it increases your soil's fertility. As a source of nitrogen, phosphorus, and potassium, it is composed of decomposing natural plant and animal debris,

such as seaweed, grass clippings, seeds, dried leaves, and tree bark, often found on the forest floor. Part of the nature of humus is that all its components have decomposed beyond recognition, forming a single mass of gelatinous

photo by Edward S. Gault

fertile material that clumps together, forming aggregates (material massed together). The aggregates are concentrated areas of soil surrounded by pockets that allow air to move around them. In this manner, air travels trough the soil and reaches the roots regularly. If you live in a more urban environment and do not have access to a backyard or trees, you may need to take a short trip to the nearest expanse of wooded parkland to claim your bounty. If you do have a yard, rake the fallen leaves from surrounding trees and keep them in a lidded barrel, which will keep them moist. Then lay them down over the soil that you have turned with a rake in the spring to feed and neutralize the dirt that will feed your fruit plants. Neutral soil is useful for growing most berry bushes and brambles.

Paper and cardboard

There are many sources of paper and cardboard for the use of organic mulch material. They are considered organic because they are made from a natural material, tree sap. If you have packing boxes, you may use these if you take all the tape off first. Shredded paper and newspaper pages that are not glossy are good sources of mulch that will benefit your plants. Lay the paper down as a thin layer between the humus and the hay, which contribute to the breakdown of the cardboard from each side. The paper and cardboard help the soil retain water and warmth, as well as the nutrients present in other mulch materials such as humus and hay, and encourages worms and insects to take up residence in the soil that surrounds the plants. This process further feeds the insects and encourages them to stay and reproduce. The insects feed the soil surrounding them with the nutrients present in their droppings. The cardboard is a neutral material that softens the acidity of the humus and bridges it to the alkalinity of the hay.

Hay and straw

Local farms and stables may sell bales of hay for you to spread over the top of your soil. In autumn, you will want to place a light layer of hay over your cover crop, if you need to plant one. This layer provides the warmth needed for the cover crop to germinate. In the spring, you will want to place a layer over the bark or peat mulch you have surrounded the base of your plants with. The hay and straw are forms of wheat grain that improve the chemical makeup of your soil. They contribute the element of carbon to the soil, which facilitates the rise in temperature created by the underground critters eating the mulch materials and adding to the nutrients present underground.

Cover crop for germination

Cover crop is the seed that you sow into your soil in the fall in preparation for the spring planting season, especially if the site has never been used for planting before, or has suffered many years of neglect. It is a form of "green manure" that increases the fertility of the soil for planting. The chemical composition of the soil is improved and the growth of weeds is suppressed. The cover crop takes the light, moisture, and nutrients away from weeds, which reduces their presence in the garden. The green growth that sprouts from the seeds is often "plowed under" instead of reaped, which means that it is turned over back into the soil with a plow. This is done so that the grain that grows is returned to the earth, and thus enhances the fertility of

photo by Karen Szklany Gault

the soil. Worms and other "critters" come out of hiding to feed on the leaves and seeds that drop off the stems after it germinates, sprouts, and falls back to the earth.

Some types of seed that you may use as a cover crop include comfrey, hairy vetch, winter rye, grazing rye, mustard, red clover, lucerne, and brassica. Legumes, such as beans, lentils, lupines, and alfalfa are often used for this purpose. They are high in nitrogen, which increases the protein content of fruits and berries. Regardless of the type of seed used, they are sown by broadcasting them. This means that they are taken up in handfuls and thrown out across the expanse of garden that needs them. They are then turned over into the soil with a garden rake. Finally, seeds are often covered with a light layer of hay, which helps to quicken the germination process by feeding the soil further and keeping the ground warm.

Bark mulch and sawdust

The bark mulch that you see in specially landscaped courtyards around office or condominium buildings is usually placed on the surface of the soil, at the base of the plant. The ground area around the plants is watered deeply so that they decompose quickly and feed the roots. Your local garden center or home improvement store would be a good source for purchasing bark mulch. Not only does it feed your soil, its presence is an attractive adornment for your garden and enhances the value or your property. It also benefits the worms, insects, and microscopic organisms that need oxygen to survive by contributing to the flow of air through the soil.

Sawdust may be added to keep oxygen flowing toward your fruit plants. Some of the other mulch materials might weigh down the soil by keeping it heavy with moisture. Sawdust is light — it absorbs nitrogen, and

it allows sufficient oxygen to reach plant roots when it is most needed. Sawdust and bark mulch work together to feed the soil for optimum fertility while providing a balanced soil environment.

photo by Karen Szklany Gault

Manures

Organic manures may be made of the feces of animals that are fed an organic diet. These include hogs and pigs, cattle such as cows and sheep, and chickens. Chickens are the most popular and accessible of these animals; they can even be raised in many city dwellers' backyards, as well as by families of rural communities. Covering piles of droppings with wood ash from the fireplace will keep chicken manure smelling sweet. Sawdust may also be used, which absorbs some of the nitrogen from the decomposition process, and softens the smell of the manure. Letting the animal manure decompose this way for nine months before use is recommended.

"Liquid" manure may be created from several sources for the purpose of covering the broadcasted seed cover in the fall. One way to create this manure is to make a piping of manure covered in burlap to create a length of fertile tubing along your garden, where it will be worked into the ground by the warmth of the sun and the pressure of rainfall. Another is to soak comfrey or nettles in a covered container then drain and lay them down when you are ready to cover your garden for the winter.

Compost

Compost is made up of the waste materials of edible substances such as fruits and vegetables, eggshells, tea leaves, and coffee grounds. Dried flowers that you have enjoyed as adornment in a vase may be given a second life as organic compost. If you live near one of the coastlines, seaweed may be harvested for this purpose. If you live in an urban environment your neighborhood florist, grocery store, or restaurant may be able to help supply you with suitable compost materials.

Organic compost is best applied to the soil in the spring and summer months, during the planting and growing seasons. Choosing the materials for amending soil for the sake of changing its pH is an important process for the fruit gardener. An alkaline soil that has a pH of 8.5 can be made more neutral with a compost of coffee grounds and pine needles. Therefore, it is important to know what the intended use of the land will be.

Kitchen waste is one of the most convenient sources of organic compost material for your soil. Examples of compostable kitchen waste include fruit and vegetable scraps, tea leaves, coffee grounds, seeds, and pits. Before kitchen waste is ready to be taken to the compost pile, it is kept in covered pails so that it will not develop an odor. The pail can be kept in the kitchen, often in a cabinet under the kitchen counter, until it becomes full. It is then emptied into an outside bin, where it continues the decomposition process and turns into nutrient-rich soil. Both the pails and the bins can be ordered online or through gardening supply catalogues. You can make your own bin by constructing a box of wooden slatted palettes. Organic waste is dumped onto the palettes, with layers of hay, sawdust, and shredded paper between the layers of compost. A layer of sand and loam is occasionally mixed in to hasten the decomposition process. To also hasten the process of transforming the compost into soil, the pile is turned over with a shovel once a week.

Green and brown compost

There are two basic types of compost materials that work together in alternate layers to create organic soil — green and brown. They each contribute vital nutrients to the soil they form together, and help keep the soil neutral. Their interaction produces heat that contributes to the decomposition process of the whole pile, and to the soil that it will be added to in order to protect it from temperature extremes.

Green matter is a source of nitrogen, which facilitates water retention. Examples of green matter include grass clippings that have not been treated with herbicide, dried weeds, manure, seaweed, alfalfa hay or meal, and food wastes, such as fruit and vegetables, coffee grounds, tea bags, and eggshells.

The layer of brown matter is a source of carbon, phosphorus, and potassium. Organic materials that are considered brown are autumn leaves, wood chips, sawdust, pine needles, straw, cornstalks, and paper. Paper can take the form of notebook or computer printer pages, shredded paper, cardboard, napkins, plates, bags, clean coffee filters, tissue, and newspaper. These materials allow air to flow through the pile, which provides the organisms that break down the green material with oxygen.

Between the layers of green and brown materials add a generous sprinkling of sawdust, or a mix of sand and loam, then turn the entire pile often with a shovel or spade to aid the flow of oxygen for the organisms that help break down the matter into soil. Using hay as one of your green materials will help sweeten the pile, preventing it from developing an odor. If you are new to creating this source of soil nutrients, it is best to start at least a year in advance to build your pile. You will need to purchase or build a bin for this purpose. You will also need a gardening shovel to turn the pile often.

photo by Edward S. Gault

The more often the pile is turned, the faster it decomposes. Keeping it moist is also important for hastening the process of decomposition. This is most often accomplished by keeping the bin door closed when the pile is not being turned. Keeping the compost bin covered also deters the intrusion of foragers, such as rats, raccoons, coyotes, and skunks.

Natural soil composition

Along with the knowledge of how dirt is created, its chemical makeup, and its texture, there is a separate factor to look at — the physical makeup of soil. Soil is basically made up of finely ground pieces of rock weathered by time and the elements — humus, water, and air. There is a natural pattern to the types of soil that exist at different layers in the earth. The top layer of soil is called topsoil. It is usually dark, made mostly of humus broken down from living materials, and carries the most nutrients for supporting plant growth. All the organisms that break down organic material live in the top layer. The next level down is the subsoil, which is drier, lighter in color, and bears fewer nutrients. It also covers more depth and needs to be fed by organic compost, seeds, and worms in order to support the growth of fruit trees and berry plants. This amendment to the subsoil is usually done when trees and other plants are set in the ground in spring. The bottom two layers are solid, sedimentary rock that is very dry and contributes no known nutrients to the growth of fruit and berry plants. The rock absorbs the water that surrounds the layers of soil above it, which increases the rate of watering needed for those layers. This is usually balanced by the addition

photo by Edward S. Gault

of the organic matter, which keeps the water closer to the roots and stems of the plants that bear fruits and berries.

Keeping grass greener

In addition to all the materials that have been listed as ingredients in topsoil humus, another source of this fertile soil is the bag full of grass clippings from lawn mowers. They may be used several ways, such as returning them to the grass as fertilizer, adding them to your compost pile, and feeding the ground around fruit trees and berry plants. They are a form of green mulch that contains nitrogen in a natural, organic form, which contributes to the rate of decomposition of other organic materials. Recycling them in this way enables you to avoid the step of bagging and disposing of the grass clippings, which would otherwise be collected by a worker in a truck. The planet is saved from extra pollutants and you benefit from having a garden and lawn that are free of chemicals.

Soil mixes

Soil mixes are created and added to soil that is already naturally present in the garden. Their purpose is to enhance the soil by adding ingredients that will improve its quality, such as changing its pH level and regulating its temperature. The soils are usually mixed in a wheelbarrow, then spread across the surface of the garden, first by hand, then worked into the ground with a garden rake. There are two basic types of soil mixes. One is the commercial mix sold in stores. The other type is organic soil that you can mix yourself, using different types of mulches. Some of the ingredients in these soils are sand, bark, peat moss, perlite mineral, and vermiculite.

> **Perlite** is crushed volcanic rock that is acidic and glassy, and takes the form of round crystals with the same chemical makeup

as obsidian. It is used to aid water drainage and the circulation of air through the soil.

Vermiculite is a smooth, glassy rock made of mica, with markings that look like worms. It is used to facilitate the retention of water and nutrients.

Peat moss (aka **Sphagnum moss**) is used to help the soil retain water.

Sand is used to facilitate the flow of air in the soil for the worms and other critters and for water drainage.

Bark mulch facilitates water retention and soil temperature moderation.

Manure is used in a dry, powdery form (gentler on the soil mix) for the nutrients that it bears.

Here are four recipes for different soil mixes that you can construct yourself in a wheelbarrow. Along with the recipe is a note about the quality that the mix adds to the soil:

1. One part fine sand and two parts finely ground bark (moderates soil temperature, balances pH)

2. Equal parts peat moss, ground bark, and fine sand (increases water retention)

3. Equal parts perlite, vermiculite, and peat moss (raises acidity)

4. Two parts peat moss, one part perlite, and one part fine sand (raises acidity)

Layering of soil with mulch materials

In addition to managing the compost piles with alternating layers of green and brown materials, and applying that organic soil in the spring when you

plant your fruits and berries, there is an additional layering of mulch materials that brings long-term benefits to the soil in your garden. In the fall prior to planting your garden, it is important to layer the soil with the organic mulch ma-

photo by Edward S. Gault

terials you have collected and the seed cover you have sown. They each bring important nutrients and texture to bear on feeding your soil and the fruit trees and plants you will be growing the following season. The manure, loams, sand, and mulch materials work together to create a vital balance for your garden soil. Green materials are alternated with brown materials for this purpose.

The prescribed order for layering is the following:

1.) Broadcast a bottom layer of green organic material, such as winter seed, across the entire expanse of your garden.

2.) Over the layer of seed cover, place a mix of topsoil and manure, which are brown.

3.) On top of the brown compost, spread a layer of hay or straw.

The hay is another green layer that serves as a blanket to capture the heat generated by the lower layers, which aids the decomposition process. In the end, the intention is for all these layers to become one whole composite soil with millions of critters crawling around under the surface. Not only do the critters eat the compost and break down the desired nutrients into a form that is ready for the ground to absorb and incorporate, they actively aerate the ground, which means that they keep the air flowing by creating pockets under the ground for the air to pass through. Worms create tunnels

that serve this purpose. They create space through which water can drain through the soil. Completing the steps for soil enhancement described above each year will boost the health of your fruits and berries and make it more likely that they will bear a more abundant crop the following season.

photo by Edward S. Gault

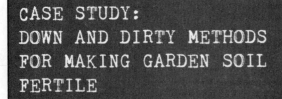

CASE STUDY:
DOWN AND DIRTY METHODS
FOR MAKING GARDEN SOIL
FERTILE

Jeff Richards is a Landscape Architect who lives and works in New England. He has been meeting with members of the Mosaic Commons co-housing community in Berlin, Massachusetts, to advise them on how best to prepare their soil organically for establishing gardens that support the growth of edible food, including fruits and berries. To Richards, compost is a living mix of naturally occurring critters — things like bacteria, fungi, earthworms, and ants — that feed on once-living organic material. The landscape architect uses it to support healthy plant growth.

"Compost creates soil that is just right for growing a desired plant or mix of plants," Richards said. The type of compost used for enhancement will affect its suitability for growing specific types of fruits and berries that prefer specific types of soil environments.

According to Richards, there are six characteristics that define soil quality: structure, mineral content, pH, water-holding capacity, drainage capacity, and fertility. "Adding compost to your soil improves all six factors," he said. The active process of the soil critters digesting the compost adds the nutrients to the ground in a way that allows the plant roots to use them to their best advantage, almost like a mother bird chewing food for her young to digest. This feeds and strengthens the plants as whole organisms, from the level of the roots.

Applying compost produced by building and tending an organic compost pile is one method that Richards uses to improve the quality of garden soil. Other methods that he favors for accomplishing this include: introducing earthworms and other microbial organisms to the soil, broadcasting a layer of cover crop over the soil followed by a layer of hay to hasten its incubation, and turning the soil to manipulate its quality and reduce weeds. Turning the soil like this mixes all the nutrients together and balances it. He uses these methods in tandem with applying compost, because he sees the composting as a "living process."

There are two major categories of compost materials — brown and green. Richards uses a formula when building a compost pile. "A ratio of 3 parts brown to 1 part green is ideal. Too much green will cause the compost pile to smell bad. If there is too much brown, the pile will not decompose very quickly." It is also a process that is done in layers. He recommends placing old corn stalks or dried tree branches across the brown layer to allow air to get into the pile. Vegetable scraps are best positioned in the center of the growing pile. "The goal is to achieve the right balance of compost materials, water, and air in order to support robust decomposing activity by the 'soil critters.'" Heat that is generated by their eating and digestive activities speeds up the rate of decomposition.

All this layering of earthy material and critter castings takes time. Patience is required to see the process through. Richards has been working with Mosaic Commons for almost a year and there is still much more to do. The soil there is rocky, has too much clay, and has been compacted by recent construction equipment. It drains poorly and some erosion has taken place. The community has carried out a variety of the soil enhancement methods that he has described above, and many more critters have been spotted around the plants that have weathered the winter months. "It is a gradual process with long-term benefits. By layering and turning the compost pile, you can produce fertility-enhancing compost in 3 to 8 months," Richards said. The community is beginning to see some fresh buds on the fruit trees and berry plants they planted last year, and is preparing to plant more this season, using compost from the piles they have been tending.

That is all the dirt about dirt. With string and stakes in your hands and a pair of sturdy boots on your feet, the moment has come to decide where you will plant each fruit and berry you will be growing this season, and to work with the earth so that the soil in your garden is fertile and ready to support them. Having the proper tools for all the gardening tasks before you will protect your back, knees, and hands. *Chapter 4 discusses some of the gardening equipment you will need for working in your garden at each stage of plant growth, from digging and raking the earth to harvesting your crops.*

CHAPTER 4

. . . .

Basic Gardening Tools You Will Need

Take a break from your adventures with dirt — catch your breath. Enjoy a quick glass of water before you take this important inventory. It is time to examine the tools you have been using to dig in the earth. If they are old and rusted, or just need to be cleaned, there is a description of how to clean them at the end of the chapter. The list of tools in this chapter is organized according to the stage in the gardening process that you will use them. If there are any essential items missing from your collection, you may want to start searching for ways to acquire them before you continue on your journey toward planting and tending your fruit garden. *Appendix A lists Web sites that offer the resources you are looking for.* Each tool has its own unique purpose for helping you make your garden grow and thrive.

DESCRIPTION OF TOOLS

. . . .

You have chosen to let your passion for gardening lead you to growing fruits and berries, and there is no turning back. Dirt lives under your fingernails, at least some of the time. Eager to grow trees or plants that will feed you and your family and friends, you are ready to take on a patch of land for the purpose of enjoying the magic of eating your favorite fruits as they ripen on the branch. Here are a few notes about some of the essential tools and other items you may want to keep in steady supply in your gardening shed. At the end of each description is an estimate of how much the item will cost to acquire.

Clothing

The first step in preparing for work in your garden is choosing what you will wear. From head to toe, your clothing will determine how comfortable you are working outside for hours at a time, and how freely you are able to move around. Perhaps it would be fun for you to set aside an outfit to wear only when you garden. You may have a mudroom or closet with a hook just for these items. Included in this outfit should be certain articles of clothing that are important for protecting your body from the effects of exposure to sun, earth, and wind.

Balms for weathered skin

If your hands do become the worse for wear, there are balms that can help soothe the aches and smooth out the rough spots. Badger Healing Balm™ is one item that you may find in organic food markets such as Whole Foods™ or Trader Joe's™. Its fragrant scent of mint is very refreshing as it is rubbed into sore, chapped skin. Olive oil, beeswax, aloe vera, and sweet birch oil are combined in one soothing gel that heals and restores hands and feet. Another type of balm that heals and smells sweeter is Nasturtium™ flower gel. Handling hay and some other types of mulch may dry out your skin despite your dedication to wearing gloves, so these gels and your favorite lotion can work in partnership with your gloves to keep your hands healthy and happy. Wearing one of them on your hands, between your skin and your gloves, may keep them young and smooth. These products usually sell for less than $8.50.

Gloves

The first item of clothing to reach for is a pair of thick, waterproof gardening gloves. If you do not yet have a pair, you may want to put them at the top of your list. Your hands will love you for that gesture of kindness. Your gloves will protect your hands while you are raking, shoveling, planting, and pruning thorny bushes. Without them, your hands could become injured, sore, chapped, or rough. Most of what you will be doing in your garden will involve using your hands, so it is important to keep them in good condition. Fortunately, gardening gloves are available in stylish colors and patterns. Online, the cost ranges from $18 to $40. At discount stores they are available for less than $10.

Kneepads

In addition to your hands, your knees need a little protection from the wear and tear they will suffer during the planting process. Wearing a layer of thick, soft material between your knees and the hard, cold ground of early spring will prevent them from becoming stiff and sore. If you wear pants while you are gardening, the kneepads will protect them from developing holes prematurely. Some gardening pants are made with kneepads. Cost range: $10 to $25.

Socks and shoes

The footwear that you don for working in your garden is as important as the gloves you wear on your hands. The skin on your feet may suffer if it is subjected to several hours of being too wet or too dry. Cotton socks are the best to wear against your skin because they will give your feet air to breathe and will absorb moisture from sweat, mud, or standing water. Waterproof boots are extra protection against moisture, or the dryness of sand. If you have a pair of hiking boots that are water-repellent, you could have them double as your gardening boots. Rubber boots offer the best protection during very wet seasons. Stylish rubber gardening boots run from $33 through QVC and $40 through the Gardener's Supply Company, to more than $100.

Sun hat

Along with your gloves, the other most important piece of clothing that is a must for an intrepid gardener like you is your sun hat. You may need to work in the heat of direct sunlight, so it is important to protect yourself from heat stroke and sunburn by wearing a hat with a wide brim. Straw and cotton will help prevent you from developing heat exhaustion. You may want to have two around, so you will always have at least one at your fingertips when the urge grabs you to tend your trees and bushes. Price range: $12 to $35.

Mapping the garden

Dressed for your gardening adventure, you are ready to make your final decisions about where in your garden you will be planting your first fruit and berry cultivars. In addition to your planning notebook and a bottle of water, you will need to use the following tools to map out and label the places where you will plant specific fruits and berries. Your decisions about their placement will determine how you will work the land to prepare the soil for growing them.

Garden line

This is the material to use when you are ready to map out exactly where in your garden you will be planting your fruit and berry cultivars. It is basically a type of string used for plotting and spacing rows of fruit plants in your garden. It is usually made of a material called polypropylene, a material that is sturdy enough to withstand weathering much better than the natural fibers that make up most strings. It is usually sold on a strong wheel for slow dispensing. It is tied by the gardener to short stakes placed at the end of each row of your garden. Average cost: $8.

Labels and permanent markers

One important aspect of being a gardener is remembering where you have planted your fruits and berries. The location you choose for your fruit plants will most likely be where they will stay for as many as ten years. It is worth making labels for them that will last just as long. These labels are more like signs, which can be made of treated wood, with the name of the plant carved in a space designated at the top, and painted with a picture of the fruit underneath. Metal, clay, and plastic will also make lasting plant labels. If you are using temporary plastic labels while the signs are being made, you will also need a collection of permanent markers that will offer clear writing, and that will last through a variety of weather conditions. Even those can be creatively rendered to look fancier, so that they add a flash of character to your garden's master plan. As soon as you have decided on the layout of your dream garden, you could use those labels to map out where you will be putting them. These types of labels are also known as "Standard Plant Markers" (Gardener's Supply Company). Cost: $15 for a set of 25.

Stakes

These are the sentinels that stand watch in your garden while you sleep, supporting all your work. Wooden stakes of varying sizes are used for different purposes in the garden, so this tool falls under several categories. The first use for stakes is mapping the garden before the planting begins. Short stakes usually stand between 3 and 5 feet in height and are used for marking the separate rows of the different types of fruits or berries you plan to plant, and hold the line used to mark the perimeters of those rows. Taller stakes are used to support the growth of fruit trees from the time they are planted, and those stand between 8 and 15 feet tall. They are usually made of chestnut, oak, or softwood that is cut from a young tree, fired in a kiln, and coated to prevent it from rotting. Softwood refers to the wood that is taken from a tree or plant in early summer, when it is growing most vigorously. This type of stake is more expensive because it lasts the longest. Metal stakes are available in bags of 25 for less than $5, or 75 for less than $10.

Digging and soil preparation

Preparing your garden soil for planting requires digging in deep to turn it and mix it up. Using only your hands would take too much time. You need tools to give you the strength for the job, while saving you time and energy. Those tools are designed to make your garden work less strenuous because they are shaped to hold the soil in specific ways, allowing you to move it efficiently.

Rake

A garden rake is heavy because it is built to stand up to rocks and hard soil, and is used to flip those rocks over while they are still in the ground. It has a long handle and four round or square prongs spaced evenly across it, with the top halves pointed down at a 90-degree angle. This tool turns the soil and mixes the different layers of dirt together, so that the nutrients spread out and feed the plants more thoroughly from the roots. It works seed cover and mulch into the layer of soil that is already there, deepening the enrichment they bring. It is also used to work compost into your garden soil in the same fashion. This type of rake is built for more durability than the average leaf rake, and known at gardening stores as a "Bow Rake." Average cost: $20.

Spade

Spade is another word for shovel. Purchasing one with a stainless steel blade will make cleaning it easier than others types of blades. Different blade shapes are used for different purposes. A round point with a beveled edge cuts through peat, roots, and hard clay dirt. The term beveled means that the head of the shovel is cut or sloped at an outward angle, with a rounded point at the top. A squared edge is used for transferring heavy, loose material, which may be useful if you plan to maintain a compost pile in an outdoor bin that will need to be turned over often. One with a narrow blade is ideal for garden transplanting and burying pipes. A spade with a rectangular shaped blade is used in a garden or nursery for turning soil and maintaining the edge to your lawn. Price range: $12 to $50.

There are three different handle shapes to watch for when purchasing a spade: the "D" shape, the "T" shape, and the standard pole shape. Handles may be made of fiberglass, wood, or stainless steel. Those that are made of fiberglass are generally stronger. One spade feature that will help prevent back strain is the presence of a "tread" on the bottom of the head. This is a small shelf that you can use to push your foot down on while anchoring your back leg so it makes a straight line with your spine and backbone.

Trowel and hand fork

They are the "dynamic duo" of gardening. The trowel and hand fork are hand-held tools for working close to the earth, such as when you would plant melon vines or strawberries. The trowel is used for digging the holes for planting, and the fork is for lifting out the roots of weeds and other undesirable material. The fork also mixes the nutrient-rich materials into the soil before you plant and water your fruit cultivars. One of the best aspects of using these tools is that they give you the chance to sit or kneel down while you work in the garden. The average price for the pair is $25.

Moving rocks and large piles of earth

The land in some gardens is very rocky, and this makes it necessary to elicit help for the heavy lifting involved in making way for plants to grow there. Removing the rocks will ensure that the roots of your plants will receive the moisture they require because rocks absorb the moisture that would otherwise benefit the plants and flowers. If your garden is not very rocky and the ground is soft enough to plant in immediately, you are a very fortunate gardener. If you do have rocks in the way of your planting, you may rent the following equipment for a specific time period, freeing your private storage space for the tools that will be used more often.

Backhoe

Some people may consider the backhoe a giant toy that poses as a landscaping and gardening tool. It is used for projects of larger magnitudes than the ordinary backyard garden, but your plans may be extraordinary. This is a machine that is operated by a human, who controls the motion of a giant, deep shovel with jagged teeth. It is a machine that is used for transporting heavy materials. One example would be to remove very rocky, claylike soil from your garden, and replace it with softer, more soluble soil. Backhoes are generally used to transport heavy loads of gravel, rocks, mulch, and loam across wide expanses of land. These machines are usually rented for a specific amount of time, because long-term storage would be challenging, especially for those who live and keep a community garden in a city, such as Boston or New York. The collected soil could be used in another location, and the rocks used to build a wall, either for privacy or as a retaining wall if your land is prone to soil erosion. You can pay a contractor to operate it for you, or have fun operating it yourself. Rental for a weekend can average $650.

Power rake

A power rake may be used to apply a top dress of sand and blend it into a large area of acidic garden soil for the purpose of neutralizing it. Also seen as a giant toy for some adults, this is a large, cylindrical tool with spiral blades, which looks much like a giant Rototiller™ without a handle. It is attached to a larger piece of machinery, such as a Bobcat™, which is a machine operated in a similar fashion to a backhoe but is wider. It is built with the means to switch attachments for different purposes. Its wheels are surrounded by a belt so that it will move as easily over grass or soil as it does on roads. This machinery is also usually rented for a limited amount of time for a specific purpose, but it is usually rented along with a contracted professional operator. It saves hours compared to turning the sand into the soil with a manual garden rake. Rental rates range from $200 to $275/day; $600 to $875/week.

Sowing and planting

When you arrive at the joyful hour of sowing the seeds or planting your first fruits and berries, you will need to use a variety of supplies fashioned for specific steps involved in those tasks. Some of those described below may be more familiar to you than others. All of them are presented here in order to help you plan what you will need, no matter which fruits you will be growing and how you will be growing them.

Budding tape

This is tape that is used as a protective cover for the site where the bud of a scion is grafted onto the host rootstock of another plant in order to produce a new cultivar. It works like a bandage so that the site will heal and begin to produce buds. Budding tape may be found at a home garden store or a nursery. *The grafting process is described in Chapter 6.* Price per roll: $3.50 to $4, depending on tape width.

Containers

If you are planning to grow some of your fruit in containers, now is the time to decide what types of containers you will need. They are made in a variety of materials, sizes, and shapes. Clay, porcelain, and stone are a few of the materials that containers are made of. You might enjoy painting one yourself at a pottery shop, such as Color Me Mine™ or The Clayground™.

photo by Edward S. Gault

Planters may also come in unique shapes, such as angels, gnomes, or gods and goddesses from classical mythology. Other places to find containers in unique shapes and textures are craft fairs and similar types of outside markets. This is one area where you have an opportunity to express your sense of style and taste. If you are growing more than one plant, you may want to choose a variety of shapes in a complementary texture and color scheme that will also match the design of your patio, deck, or balcony. If you are keeping some on windowsills inside your home, you may want to match them to the color scheme of the rooms they will adorn. One of the most important aspects of choosing containers is that they are big enough for the plants you will be growing in them to establish deep roots and produce a healthy batch of lush foliage and blossoms. Some people like to use a batch of smaller containers, while others like to use bigger ones such as tubs to grow more of their favorite fruits or berries. Recycled food containers, such as gallon jugs, may work for you. You will also need a marker and a handful of plastic labels to identify into which containers you have sown each of your plants. *The steps for growing fruits and berries in containers are discussed in greater detail in Chapter 6.* They range in price from $10 to $50, depending on the size, shape, and texture of the pot. Some are sold in pairs or groups at various prices. Large, self-watering patio containers cost an average of $40.

Irrigation equipment

After sunshine, the second most important resource to your fruits and berries is water. The ability to walk to any point in your garden with your hose and give them a drink will make giving them ongoing care both possible and joyful. An outside faucet is vital for regular watering. A hose to attach to the faucet at one end and a sprinkler at the other will give you the breadth of movement needed to reach all of your plants with the water they need. A spray nozzle attached at the end of the hose might reach even farther. Attaching a metal watering wand with a wide-spraying nozzle to the hose will also allow you to bring the source of water a greater distance with its far-reaching spray. Classic garden wands are usually about 30 inches long, and the length of patio wands is closer to 16 inches. Another variation is made especially for watering hanging plants. For an additional source of water, you can use a watering can. As with the wand, there are a wide variety of shapes of watering cans available. One type is called a "Haws can," named after the Englishman who invented it in 1886. It contains a spill shield at its neck and a long, thin spout, attached to the neck by a bar on top. The bar offers an extra grip for holding the can, and thus extra control for maneuvering. There is another that works especially well if you are growing some of your fruit plants in containers on your patio. It is called a "container," or "conservatory," watering can. Another type of can is made especially for watering seedlings, and another for watering roses. A 50 ft. hose costs about $10. Slim lightweight hoses range from $45 to $65.

A pivoting watering wand can cost $16.95. A tall sprinkler with a far reach is about $45. The Haws model mentioned above is available in plastic for less than $30, as are others that have long-reaching spouts.

Knife

Knives are used for grafting the wood of plants for the creation of new cultivars. The size used by gardeners is generally 3 ½ inches in length and has a straight blade. Both the scion and the rootstock are stripped of bark so that the soft wood underneath is visible. A hole is made in the wood of the host plant, into which is inserted a branch of the scion, so that they eventually become part of each other in order to create a new plant. *The entire grafting process is described in Chapter 6.* Price range: $16.50 to $22.50; a kit with more pieces costs about $70.

Raised beds

There is no reason to wait an extra year to grow your favorite fruits and berries. Raised beds are often used for fruit, herb, and vegetable gardening, especially when the soil needs extra encouragement to support plant growth. They are sold in kits that are simple to assemble and fill with healthy loam for sowing and planting. Eartheasy is one website that sells them and can be found at **www.eartheasy.com**. The price range for the beds that they sell is $79 to $450.

Rototiller™

This popular tool is mainly used for applying lime to highly acidic soil or applying fertilizer to the soil of plants that require its ongoing application. It has a long handle and a horizontal, cylindrical rolling blade that works the lime or fertilizer into the soil. The time it saves makes it a worthy investment. If you plan to grow citrus trees, bramble berries, or bush berries, this will be one of your most important pieces of equipment. Price range: $30 for simple, light tiller to more than $1,000 for one that is electric.

Seed trays

You will need seed trays for sorting and incubating your seeds for planting. Plastic trays are inexpensive and recyclable. Some are made with compartments so that each seed may be planted in its own soil and kept on your windowsill to germinate. Others are trays without compartments in which soil blocks are created and stored — the soil-blocking machine is described below. You can buy such a machine at a garden center or nursery, or create one yourself with recycled materials. One example of this would be to plant the seeds into the wells of egg cartons that have not held broken eggs. This would be a great way to recycle Styrofoam™, which is not biodegradable. It is easier to clean with a damp, soapy sponge than a cardboard carton would be. Once the cartons are clean, you may place potting soil in the separate compartments. After a small hole is made in each well of soil, dip a toothpick in water and use it to transfer one seed into the hole in the middle of each soil-filled compartment of the Styrofoam™ carton. Finally, create a label identifying what fruit the seeds are meant to grow with a Sharpie™ marker on a small strip of masking tape. The label can be placed on the side of the carton, where it is most easily visible. The simplest way to organize them would be by making each row of wells one type of seed. The average cost of 1 tray that will hold about 80 soil blocks is $13.

Soil blocker

The soil blocker, or soil block maker, is a block of 20 square holes with a handle on top for the gardener to hold. It is a simple machine that squeezes a pile of loam together into blocks, and simultaneously makes the impressions to place

photo by Karen Szklany Gault

the seeds in. One seed is placed in each hole to grow a seedling. A small, four-block maker is $30. A large, commercial 20-block maker is $200. Both are sold online at the Johnny Seeds website.

Sprayer

A sprayer usually comes in the form of a can with a short hose extending from one side. It may be used to fertilize the leaves and soil of seedlings grown in a cold frame *(see Chapter 6, under "Greenhouse Growing")*. It may also be used to apply stored pollen onto the flowers of plants that need it because they do not have an appropriate pollen-producer that would do so naturally growing nearby, *(see Chapter 5, under "Artificial Pollination")*. Average price: $30.

Tree ties

Tree ties are used to hold the tree in place between two stakes in order to support its vertical growth when it is newly planted. Materials generally used to make these ties include strips of cotton shirts, canvass, strong rope cord, bicycle tires, and even thin chains. The strongest trees need the material of rubber bicycle tires or chains, depending upon what stage of growth they are in when you buy or plant them. Medium strength starts at $11/ roll and high strength starts at $30/roll. Stretch rolls start at $1.70/roll. Tree staking kits run from $12 to $20.

Wood, hammer, and nails

If you take pleasure in making your own containers, you know that these three items will serve you in all of your building endeavors. Wood planks of various sizes, a strong hammer, and many nails will allow you to build seed trays, cold frames, incubation tables, stakes for supporting trees and plants when they are needed, and even hive boxes for keeping honeybees. *More details about how to do that are discussed in Chapter 5.* Some fruit plants, such as melon vines, need to spend time in cold frames in early spring to keep them warm so that they adapt to the climate they will be grown in before they are planted in the ground, and to protect them from the threat of soil erosion. In some circumstances, you may need to grow berries in raised beds and might want to build them yourself. The amount of wood you will need depends on the size of the parcel of garden you plan to devote to these fruits. Some gardeners have built their own wooden seed trays using these materials. Others create greenhouses from a wooden base. You can also build yourself a makeshift, sturdy tree support if you need more than just your own two hands for a planting project. For such a tool, two strips of wood can be nailed together at a right angle with the hammer to create a support for a dormant fruit tree cultivar that you are ready to plant. One of the pieces would span the distance between the place where the tree will be planted and the edge of the hole that you have dug for the tree. The other would be as tall as the tree. The tree would be tied to this piece with rope or garden line to hold it in place and provide it with a surface to rest against. This wood support offers you a set of improvised hands to support the tree while you finish stretching out the roots and preparing the hole for filling in. *The use of wooden cold frames, greenhouses, and raised beds for planting and growing fruits and berries will be discussed in greater detail in Chapter 6.* Hammers are available for less than $20. A small package of nails costs less than $5. The price of wood varies according to size, grain, weight, etc. The wood for a raised bed would cost less than $100.

Pruning

The weather is warmer than it was when you first planted your fruits and berries. Your trees and bushes have developed buds that have become off-shoot branches, leaves, and flowers. Once your trees begin to grow, they will need to be cut back to make sure that only the most prolific branches grow out. Different types of pruning tools are needed for the pruning process, depending on when it will be done, and the maturity of the plant that is being pruned. There are a variety of tools for getting the job done, such as shears, pruners, and loppers. Read on to learn the differences between them.

Ladders

Ladders are useful for both pruning trees and harvesting fruit from them. Aluminum ladders fashioned after a tripod are stable and can be used with fruit trees up to 15 feet high. One example of this is the 3-legged orchard ladder, which is recommended by Roger Swain of the PBS series *Victory Gardens* as the safest to use. It is available at heights of 6 ft. and taller. There is often a rail for leaning against and a ledge to support a pail or barrel for holding harvested fruit. For your safety, it is important to make sure the branch you place the ladder near can withstand the weight of both the ladder and you before leaning against it. The orchard ladder mentioned above starts at $116 online, at *Ladder King*.

Long-arm pruners

Long-arm pruners are one in the family of pruners that are used to cut back unproductive branches of fruit trees and bushes. Their main distinction is that they have longer handles. Using these might save you from being scratched by bramble thorns or sharp, skinny branches, because they allow you to stand farther back when pruning. Price range: $30 to $117.

Loppers

Loppers have a thicker blade and bigger handles than regular pruners. They are used to cut thicker branches, closer to the center of the fruit tree or berry plant. Because this type of pruning requires the gardener to get up close and personal with the plants, it may be best to wear your gloves, a shirt with long sleeves, and long pants, all of which will protect the skin of your hands, arms, and legs from being scratched. Price range: $20 to $60.

Pole pruners

This tool is a pruner that sits on top of a pole, which is longer than long-arm pruners. It is often equipped with a saw that will help cut thicker branches. The main advantage of these pruners is that they reduce the time spent on a ladder. Price range: $68 to $130.

Saw

Sometimes special pruning saws are needed to cut in places that are awkward to reach that long-arm pruners cannot cut. They are useful to you if you do not like climbing ladders and need to cut branches that have a diameter wider than 2 inches. Pruning saws are lightweight and are available in a variety of shapes. The tri-cut edge is the most widely recommended, because its cut is smoothest and its motion the least strenuous. Some may be folded and have a 7-inch blade. A saw with a 3-inch blade can cut a branch as thick as 10 inches in diameter. A pruning saw may be purchased online for as little as $12.

Shears

Pruning shears are basically scissors with a special handle. They have short heads and handles, and are used to prune away thin branches of the outer growth of trees and bushes. Different types of shears are shaped for pruning different types of growth. The most common types are flowers, grass, thinning, and hedge shears. If some of your berry bushes function as hedges, it would be wise to invest in shock-absorbing handles and wavy blades that hold branches as well as cut them. Price range: $10 to $54.

Protection from pests and diseases

Once your trees and bushes begin forming fruit and that fruit begins to ripen, there will be furry, four-legged creatures, such as raccoons and squirrels, who will want a sample or two. The supplies described below can be used to discourage their invasion of your garden, so that you will have enough fruit left to turn into jams and pies when the peak season for harvesting them arrives.

You can make your own tree guards that keep furry scavengers from eating both blossoms and fruit. Garden centers or hardware stores have 1-inch thick mesh wire that you can purchase and cut to make a cylindrical barrier around your tree or plant. This way, you will be able to keep animals away from your plants, preventing any destruction that could come from these creatures. You may also want to place some lighter mesh wire over your berry bushes so that the birds will wait until they are ripe before they enjoy their feast. There are also plastic tree guards that come already made. They will have to be pushed into the earth and the soil matted down firmly around them in order for them to stay in place. *The subject of protecting your crops from scavengers and other pests will be discussed further in Chapter 8.* Organic gardening guards run from $3.50 to $30, depending on the size of the mesh; sold in packs of 5.

Harvesting equipment

For the most part, your hands will be your main harvesting tools. You will want to wear your gloves when browsing through thorny plants, and you will need a bucket nearby for storing the harvest you will be gathering. When you harvest from fruit trees, you will need either a ladder (see description under the section above labeled Pruning) to stand on, or a picking tool that will allow you to stand on the ground. This is a long pole with a basket attached at the top, designed for harvesting tree fruit. Collecting fruit by standing in the back of a pickup truck might allow you to gather a cornucopia of fresh fruit, because the space allows for filling a large group of baskets at the same time. The pole picker tool is available online for $5.99, used and up to $25, new.

CARE AND MAINTENANCE OF GARDENING TOOLS FOR THE WINTER MONTHS

When you are finished using your tools for the season, there are steps you can take to keep them clean and free of rust so that they continue to serve your gardening projects for many years. Those steps are presented below.

1. Brush the metal heads of your tools with sand. This will dry them off, removing excess water, grease, and miscellaneous debris.

2. Soak a cotton rag in a mild bleach solution and wipe the metal down to protect them from attack by rust or other parasites.

3. Coat them with mineral oil, which also gives them extra protection from rust throughout the long winter months of storage and nonuse.

4. Install hooks in your garage, shed, basement, or other cool, dry place in your home. Hanging the tools on these hooks will keep them from scratching one another. A tool hanging kit with hooks may be purchased online for $35.

Tool safety

In addition to the care you give to your tools, be mindful of the care that your hands also need when working with them. Sharp tools with safety latches need to be stored and transported while they are latched, and kept inaccessible to young children. Wearing your gardening gloves while storing and transporting them will give your hands added protection from injury.

The description of tools and other gardening supplies presented above is a sampling of what is used at each stage of the adventure of growing fruits and berries. They may be acquired at home improvement stores, hardware stores, the Internet, or friends who no longer garden. You may find some tools available through your local online "Freecycle" network, at **www. freecycle.org**. This is a site that offers an opportunity for you to give away things you no longer use in exchange for acquiring things that you have discovered a need for. From this website you may join a local group of "freecyclers" to trade treasures with. Once you have checked your list and

have determined that you have everything you need to start growing your fruits and berries, it is time to move on to the next step. *Chapter 5 discusses how the pollination needs of your plants will determine how many you will grow, and where in your garden you will plant them to ensure a cornucopia of ripe fruit at harvest time.*

Pollination

The time has arrived for a discussion about the birds and the bees. It is pretty incredible to discover that flowers have sex lives. It is important to understand what makes particular plant species grow back over the course of hundreds of years, even millennia. This discovery will make a big difference in how you approach the process of choosing which fruit varieties to plant and grow in your garden. The responsibility for all this evolution falls on a grain smaller than a mustard seed. Pollen is the magic dust that makes the proliferation of all flowering plant species possible, and makes it possible for those that produce edible food to do just that. It contains the sex cells (gametes) of the flowers that blossom and form fruit. Most flowers are formed with both male and female parts to their anatomy. Just like in humans, the male parts (stamens) produce male gametes that are carried by a substance that must make contact with the female parts (pistils), so that the seeds will form for new flowers of that species to develop on the plant and bloom. That substance is the pollen.

After the pollen makes contact with the pollen-receiving pistil, it creates a hole in the stigma and sends a tube with a male gamete down the stile, toward the ovules in the green receptacle area at the bottom of the flower blossom. It is called the receptacle because its main function is to accept the male gametes into the ovules, where the female gametes are stored. When the male gametes meet the female gametes, fertilization occurs. This union produces the seeds that become new plants that grow the same type of flower. The seeds are carried by the wind to another spot on soil that is hopefully moist enough for it to germinate. If this is true, a new plant will grow.

The transfer of pollen is made by an insect or animal called a pollinator. The wind, and even water, can be instrumental in transporting the pollen

from the stamens to the pistils. So are the bees. They are the most well known pollinators in history. Honeybees are the predominant pollinator of the bee family, but other bees, such as the bumblebee and carpenter bee, also perform this service. Hummingbirds are a close second to the bees, as are the fruit bat and the Australian honey possum. They all drink the sweet juice found at the base of the flower, called nectar, which contains many nutrients that the insects and animals need. The fragrance of the nectar is how the flowers attract their pollinators to them. This is the tip that the pollinators receive for their pollen deliveries. When bees visit the flower to extract the nectar, the pollen made by the stamens clings to their fur, feathers, legs, or wings. If a plant is self-pollinating, the bee needs only to move to another flower on the same plant and brush up against its pistils for fertilization to occur.

If cross-pollination between two varieties of the same plant species is necessary, the bee must fly between flowers of the two plants in order to transfer the pollen from the stamens of one variety to the pistils of the other, and then do the same in the other direction. The cross-pollinating plants must be placed in close proximity to one another for the cross-pollination to occur. For this process to be as successful as possible, it is important to note which species of fruit plants play the role of pollinator, which is a term that is also applied to a plant that produces pollen that fertilizes certain compatible recipient plants. Fruit flowers, as many others, are very picky about the partners with whom they produce children. The male cells encased in the pollen will only fertilize the female cells of certain fruit flower varieties, but not all. If it senses an inappropriate receptor, it will not send down the tube with the male gamete through the pistil. Nursery staff who know the growing history, habits, and needs of the plants and flowers they work with will be able to help you determine which varieties of fruit trees are best grown close to each other for their optimal productivity.

Before digging in and breaking ground, it is important to choose the varieties of fruits and berries you would like to plant, keeping their pollination needs in mind in addition to other qualities you are attracted to. There are many options to choose from. With careful placement and maintenance, your plants will flower and grow abundant fruit, but they may need your knowledgeable partnership in the process.

Some plants, such as those that grow on brambles, are primarily self-pollinating and just need the attention of the bees, or the wind, to transport pollen from the stamens of one flower to the pistils of another flower on a single berry bush.

Others, such as apples and other tree fruits, have both male and female varieties that need to be planted near one another so that cross-pollination between them can happen. Cross-pollination involves the transportation of pollen between the stamens of the flowers of one plant and the pistils of flowers on another. In this way, both are fertilized and can produce fruit. Keeping those that depend on cross-pollination close to their source of fertilization will ensure an abundant crop at harvest.

A third type of pollination, which is usually done by the gardener, is artificial pollination. This process is necessary when one of the fruit trees needed for cross-pollination becomes sick and dies, or when not enough honeybees visit the garden to drink the nectar from the fruit-producing flowers. The gardener must take the pollen from the stamens of one plant and place it on the pistils of the other manually. There are various ways to do this, which are described in a later section of this chapter, titled Artificial Pollination.

The following section presents in detail the parts of the flower involved in the process of pollination, which results in fertilization, seed production, and fruit formation.

ANATOMY OF A FRUIT FLOWER

Here is a review of how the parts of a flower work together to procreate, while also creating fruit that will ripen into naturally healthy tasty treats. The most important ingredient in the process of pollination is the pollen. Pollen is a sticky powder found in the stamens at the center of flowers, which contains the male sex cells of the flower. It may be red, brown, yellow, or orange. Pollination occurs when pollen from the anthers of the stamen is transferred to the stigma of another flower. The stamen is the male, pollen-*producing* part of the flower, located in the center, surrounded by the petals. It has two main parts: the anther and the filament. The anther is the head of the stamen. The filament is a long, very thin stem that the anther is attached to. The pistil is the female, pollen-*receiving* part of the flower. The tip of the pistil is called the stigma. The long, thin fibrous stem of the pistil is called the style. It is very thin and shorter than the stamens that surround it and is also located in the center of the flower. All of these parts are joined together by the base, or receptacle, of the flower, which contains the ovules on either side of the style. The ovules contain the ovaries, which produce the seeds and fruit.

This fertilization produces the seeds that become the flowers and fruit. Fruits that have one seed, or pit, such as peaches and plums, need only one grain of pollen to fertilize the female sex cells in their ovaries. The apple has seven seeds and needs seven grains of pollen for full fertilization and the

development of healthy flowers and fruit. When choosing which plants to buy, it is important to obtain a good pollinating variety, which is a fruit tree or berry plant that produces enough pollen for cross-pollination with others.

photo contributed by Martin Miller

SELF-POLLINATING PLANTS

Most berries are self-pollinators. This means that they have the capacity to pollinate and bear fruit without the presence of another berry plant growing nearby. Brambles such as raspberries and blackberries are good examples of this. One tree fruit that is self-fruitful is the sour cherry. The pollen produced by their stamens fertilizes the pistils of other flowers on the same plant. The pollen is carried on the wind, by a bee, or by a hummingbird.

Citrus trees usually self-pollinate or rely on the insects for pollination, but the flowers that develop often fall off before the tree has a chance to bear fruit. The tree must be sufficiently warm and moist for the blossoms to stay on the branches. It is natural for some citrus fruits to form without the pollination of the flowers on the tree; This results in fruit that is seedless. Somehow, the process of sexual reproduction occurs without the fertilization that occurs through pollination, which is referred to as parthenogenesis. Another word used for this process is parthenocarpy, which pertains to

fruit flowers that are not pollinated, so that they bear fruit without seeds. It may take five to 18 months for the fruit to begin developing after the flowers fall from the tree.

CROSS-POLLINATING PLANTS

Most tree fruit and some berry plants are cross-pollinators, meaning that they need to be planted with another tree — one that is a different variety of the same species that blooms at the same time. Two or three different compatible varieties of one type of fruit are usually clustered in one particular section of a garden. Not all varieties of the same species of trees are good pollen-producing varieties. Some varieties are better than others. It is important to pay attention to this detail so that you plant a good pollen-producer in with poor ones. Closely related varieties will not pollinate well with each other, so it is important to plant varieties of fruit trees that are unrelated to one another for good fruit production. This is especially true for varieties of apples, peaches, pears, plums, sweet cherries, pecans, hazelnuts (filberts), Carpathian walnuts, butternuts, blueberries, and elderberries. Some of these trees depend more on one form of cross-pollination than others. Pecans depend more on the wind than the bees. Honeybees are very important to apples, pears, and avocados. The staff members of your local nursery or horticultural society are likely to be your most knowledgeable sources and can help you choose a customized cadre of cross-pollinators to plant in your garden. Careful attention at this stage of the process will save you time and energy, because the alternative to matching the appropriate cross-pollinators with each other is the necessity of pollinating your fruit flowers artificially.

ARTIFICIAL POLLINATION

There are times when gardeners are required to take a more active role in the pollination process. Artificial pollination is a version of the pollination process that is completed by human hands instead of being left to natural forces. These trees will not flower or bear fruit unless you help the process along, usually because a fruit tree that depends on cross-pollination has been planted with an incompatible pollinating variety growing nearby, or without any other pollinator in close proximity. Perhaps a lack of available space prohibits growing more than one type of fruit tree in your garden. Some trees are just more vulnerable to late frosts if they have not yet been pollinated and need the extra help from the gardener for their survival until a cross-pollinator can be purchased and planted nearby. During the interim period, the gardener may need to pollinate this type of tree artificially.

There are different methods of artificial pollination. One method for manual artificial pollination is placing a branch of a flowering tree in water under the tree that needs pollination and letting the bees take up the rest of the cross-pollination process from there. Another method is known as grafting. This involves taking the bark or limb of a compatible variety of tree and attaching it to one of the limbs or roots of your own tree. This method is labor-intensive and requires extensive knowledge of the growing habits, hardiness, and environmental sensitivities of the fruit species you would like to grow. Each species has its own grafting procedure requirements. *If you are ambitious enough to try grafting, the process is described in greater detail in Chapter 6.*

Other orchardists collect pollen from the strong pollinators with a vacuum and spray it on those that are poor pollinators. Some have bought bags of pollen at a nursery or gardening store and placed the pollen in a beehive, so that the bees cannot help but to collect the pollen on their bodies and distribute it randomly along their daily route.

Finally, there is direct hand pollination. This is the method that you would most likely use if you find the need to artificially pollinate your charges. It is a form of artificial pollination that involves brushing pollen off flowers that produce it in abundance and brushing it onto those that do not. For this form of pollination, pollen is brushed off the stamens of pollinating tree blossoms into a cup with a camel-hair paintbrush, and brushed onto the pistils of blossoms that have not been pollinated. You may need to search for an appropriate pollen-producer, particularly if there are no other trees with a variety of the same fruit you are growing within a three-mile radius. This is the radius of travel for a colony of bees on a pollination flight. With the Colony Collapse Disorder (CCD) crisis affecting so many bee colonies, the need for such artificial pollination measures has increased. Some examples of fruit flowers that may need this help from you are apples, peaches, pears, pistachios, sour cherries, blueberries, and elderberries.

If you are growing some of your fruit in a greenhouse, the trees and bushes will not receive the same exposure to the wind and bees as those that grow in an outside garden. This will make it necessary for you to hand-pollinate them. Some tropical fruit plants, such as the yellow passion fruit, may need help with productivity through hand pollination, because some of the natural pollinators for such plants might not be sold in the United States. If this is true, your local horticultural society staff should be able to help you find a compatible cross-pollinator that would accept the pollen of your fruit plant, or from which your fruit plant will accept pollen.

Spring is usually the best time to pollinate the flowers of fruit trees — whenever they begin to blossom and pollen is visible on their stamens. This is a simple process that a child may delight in helping to complete.

Steps in the Hand-Pollination Process:

1. Brush the middle of the fruit flowers on the designated "pollinator" plant with a ½-inch or 1-inch camel hair paintbrush.

2. Store the brush in a plastic storage bag.

3. Using a marker and masking tape, label the bag with the name and variety of the fruit plant the pollen was collected from.

4. Refrigerate the collected pollen overnight if it is not transferred immediately.

> 5. As soon as possible after brushing, so that the gametes do not die, apply the pollen to the middle of the flowers on the plant or plants that need pollination.

Each of the pollination methods described above offers a fabulous opportunity for gardeners to be partners with nature in the life cycle of the fruit plants they are growing. The more types of fruit included in each garden, the greater the variety offered for the enjoyment of bee colonies that have adapted and survived; from that variety, they will grow stronger. The result is a garden of trees, bushes, and vines that will yield an abundant harvest of delicious fruit for many years.

KEEPING BEES

One way to ensure the healthy pollination of your fruit trees and berry bushes is to keep your own colony of honeybees. They are such beautiful creatures, especially when their wings reflect the sunshine on a summer afternoon. Their busy buzz has a musical quality to it. The design of the combs that they create follows a mathematical progression, discovered by a twelfth century Italian mathematician named Leonardo Fibonacci. The design of the sunflower works the same way, and bees love the nectar of sunflowers, just as they love that of flowers grown to bear fruit. Working together, bee colonies are groups of overachievers. They usually produce more honey than they need, and are prone to swarming only if there is more honey produced than they can consume, therefore making it difficult for them to move around their home. This is preventable by supplying extra surface space for them to build honeycombs on. It is also easily remedied by taking an unoccupied hive box and holding it by the tree they are occupying. They will eventually land on the frame to rest and begin to build a new hive on it. Contrary to popular belief, swarming bees are the most docile and easiest to tame because they are full of honey. Being so full, they cannot move in a manner that is effective for stinging.

There is a give and take to the relationship between honeybees and humans. You ensure the strength of a bee colony when you give them the opportunity to drink the delicious nectar from a variety of flowers during the warmer months. In return, they ensure the best production of fruits and berries from your trees and bushes. Not only will you be rewarded with an abundance of sweet fruit to eat, but you will also enjoy fresh honey for your tea,

photo contributed by Becky Pulito

pancakes, waffles, madelines, and other tasty treats. This is one reason why the present might be the best time to begin keeping bees. The crisis of CCD has caused a decline in the national bee population, and the future of the availability of healthy food crops depends on their return.

Beekeeping for pollination and sustainability

Becky Pulito is a seasoned beekeeper who lives in New England with her family. She kept three colonies of Italian honeybees between 2003 and 2008. "The Italian bees are generally considered the most productive and docile, but they are not the hardiest of the species," she said. "I lost one colony the first year and split my other two hives to fill that one. A couple of years later I lost two, but did not split my third hive. In 2008 my third hive died."

In 2009, she moved into Camelot Cohousing in Berlin, Massachusetts, and has already ordered her bees for the upcoming spring season.

She is considering Russian bees for her next beekeeping adventure. "They are more cold-hardy than the Italian bees." She expects them to survive the period of clustering better during the colder months of New England.

When asked how she orders her bees, she said, "I like to order a nucleus hive. It has an established brood comb and the rest of the colony is happy with their queen." She estimated that her most recent order averaged to about $200 a hive for just the equipment. A basic package of bees costs about $75 and contains 9,000 bees, weighing 3 pounds, with an average of 3,000 bees per pound. The nucleus hive contains the same amount of bees, but costs $125 because of the sugar plug. Pulito considers the head start given to her by ordering that type of package worth the higher price. "Bees generally cost more now because they are in greater demand, due to Colony Collapse Disorder," she said.

Her last hive of bees was kept in her backyard, facing away from her house, against a fence. On her property grew raspberry canes and crabapple trees, which were very productive plants because of the proximity of busy pollinators. Their flight path crossed her driveway, but she was never stung for that reason. "The stings have come from handling the frames to check on the hives or to harvest their honey." The protective clothing she wears when working with the bees includes a bee jacket, a hood with a veil, and a pair of gloves.

She is considering a line of trees to the north of her cohousing village as the next home for her bees. "This will give them plenty of dappled sunlight," Pulito said. It will be the perfect spot for both keeping an eye on them and letting them freely pollinate the surrounding flora, which includes a variety of fruits and herbs.

Not interested in using some of the methods that other beekeepers employ to manage their colonies, Pulito will not feed them sugar water, but will either leave them more of their own honey beginning in late summer, or give them back their honey if they run out in the winter. She also allows them to decide when to re-queen; she does not interfere with that process, either.

"I do not like to over-manage the colonies. They adapt better to their environment when they are left to manage their hive themselves," she noted. She just checks on them in the winter and makes sure they are well fed.

Pulito also makes sure they are dry enough in the winter, when moisture has a tendency to pool in the hives. "Moisture kills them, so I learned to leave the top of the hive box propped open during the day in the winter, so the wind can help keep them dry. They are not as bothered by the cold." When asked how she uses the honey she does harvest and store, she said that her family enjoys eating it on English muffins and cream cheese. She likes to make lotions and bath soaps for her friends to enjoy.

Pollination is a pretty mighty subject. Without it, there would be no gardens to grow and no fresh, delicious food to eat. If you want your garden to be the bee's knees, there are more juicy details to consider for keeping your hive buzzing with ripe fruit. *Read on to Chapter 6 to find out how best to plant, feed, and water your new trees and bushes.*

photo contributed by Martin Miller

CHAPTER 6

• • • • • • • • • • • •

Cultivation and Planting

The time has finally arrived for the planting to begin. It is the moment you have been diligently preparing for, the next step toward making the garden you have been dreaming of. If the late frosts of spring are behind you and the days have gotten warmer and the ground has softened, it is time to lay out your tools and start digging the holes that will welcome your fruit plants and encourage them to spread their roots. The first items you will need are your sun hat, gloves, spade, kneepads, and a tape measure. Planting is a process that involves great dedication and patience. Providing your trees and plants with a healthy place to grow roots and later produce fruit takes time to measure, dig, cover with fertile soil, add compost and mulch, and irrigate deeply.

If you are ordering some of your fruit trees from a catalog, keep in mind that some nurseries send their trees out bare-rooted with no extra covering for protection and moisture. These trees need extra care. It is best to unwrap them upon arrival, keep them in a basement or a similarly warm environment, and let them soak in water for four or five hours. You will want to plant these trees in the spring, because their roots are vulnerable to a late frost. Trees and plants that are purchased or arrive by mail with a covering of soil, called a soil plug, are not so fragile. Read the catalog or call the seller to find out what his or her shipping habits are, and plan the timing of your order to coincide closely with your intended planting schedule.

This chapter is your guide to the process of diving into the earth to prepare it for receiving your fruit plants, feeding their roots healthy nutrients so that they will develop healthy root systems, covering the roots with the soil you have dug up, and watering them so that they will grow to produce the fruit you are looking forward to eating. Each fruit species, and subspecies, will have individual needs. For example, trees will need to be planted further apart than bushes. Melon vines will need to be cultivated from seeds and trained in groups of four along rows of soil in wooden cold frames before they are planted into the ground. Grape vines will need to be trained around trellises for support. Rows of strawberries will need to be plotted with garden line and spaced apart to allow enough room for each plant to flourish without blocking the growth of another.

Different types of fruit are best planted at different stages in tree or plant development. Some need to be planted from seeds. Others are propagated in a container and then planted in the spring as dormant rootstocks, which refers to the roots of the tree and a few inches of the trunk above them. Some weaker varieties may need to be grafted onto tougher host rootstocks to produce a cultivar for a tree that will both survive the transplanting process and produce delicious fruit. The branch of the weaker variety is known as the scion, which refers to the trunk, branches, leaves, and fruit of that tree. The grafting is done before the cultivar is planted, so the steps involved in the grafting process are described first in this chapter. It is included for those of you who are ambitious enough to try your hand at it, instead of buying one from a nursery.

GRAFTING

Grafting trees is also called "budding," because a bud from the tree that the gardener desires to propagate (scion) is inserted into the bark of the host tree (rootstock). The method called the "T" budding procedure is the simplest, and the one recommended for inexperienced growers. You will need a knife with a 3 ½-inch straight edge.

The first step in the process is to select the variety of fruit you would like to cut a bud from. It needs to be healthy and strong enough to endure the rigors of cutting, grafting onto another tree, and planting. You will want to check with your local horticultural society or your state house about whether the species you want to plant is banned in your area due to the diseases it may carry. It is important to check if the budwood is imported from another state or from an area in your own state that may be considered "quarantined." Budwood is the wood of a fruit tree from which a bud will be grafted onto another variety of the same species.

Once you have found the scion that you are looking for, follow these simple steps:

1. Take a branch from the desired species of tree (scion) that is well endowed with buds and has begun to harden. This is best done during the natural growth period of the tree, normally between April and November. But it is best not to use the first buds of the season, which may damage the tree it is taken from, and the buds may be too young to survive the process.

2. Trim the branch down to a length of 8 to 12 inches with the straight-edged knife. It is important to use this scion as soon as

possible, so the third step is to choose a young and hardy tree that you will be using as the host rootstock variety.

3. Make a one-inch vertical cut, then a horizontal cut below it, which together look like an inverted "T" on the trunk of the host tree, about 6 inches above the ground.

4. Cut a bud, along with a one-inch sliver of wood, from the scion. Then insert it completely into the flap of the "T," where the two cuts meet.

5. Wrap the graft with budding tape. Begin below the site, wrapping the trunk several times below the graft, overlapping each layer.

6. Keep wrapping until you have reached the spot where there are several rounds of wrap above the graft site. The budding tape should be removed from the graft site no more than 30 days after it has been applied. A green, healthy-looking bud will indicate a successful graft.

7. Force growth of the grafted bud to stimulate the growth of the union. To do this, cut 2/3 of the way through the trunk of the rootstock, at about 1½ inches above the graft union, on the same side as the union. Then lay the rootstock on the ground. After there has been 3 to 4 inches of growth from the

photo by Karen Szklany Gault

union, the top of the host rootstock can be cut off, from about 1½ inches above the grafted bud.

To encourage continued growth of the grafted union, buds that originate from other places on the rootstock should be cut off, so that competition from them is discouraged. Now the grafted rootstock is ready to be planted. Trees grafted onto seedlings that are expected to grow to full height are planted so that the graft union is kept just below the soil line when the hole is re-filled. The graft union on the seedling of a dwarf tree variety is kept 2 to 3 inches above the soil line.

PLANTING TREE FRUITS

There are certain attributes of propagated cultivars that you can purchase from a nursery, either directly or online, that make them more likely candidates for adjusting successfully to a new growing environment. You will

want to work with a tree that is at least one year old, has a straight trunk of about ½ to ¾ inch in diameter, measures four to five feet high, and has evenly spaced branches. A tree with these characteristics has had time to grow in a particular climate, and therefore adapt to it. That growing environment will be the same as your own if you are purchasing the tree from a local nursery. A tree that has been grown for a period of time in the ground outside has become acclimated to the temperature ranges of the soil and is more likely to survive the process of transplanting.

The tree might be able to adjust better to its new soil environment if it is planted while it is still dormant. The most common season to plant is spring, when the ground is soft and not heavy with moisture. If the ground is too moist, it might be too heavy and has the potential to suffocate the roots and kill the plant.

1. Dig a hole for planting your tree. The hole should be twice as big as the ball of roots at its base. When determining the depth of the hole, it is also important to know whether the tree you will be planting has been grafted. For a tree that will grow to the average height for its species, you will want to take into account that the graft union will need to lie just beneath the soil line you will be creating. If the tree is a dwarf species, the graft union will need to lie 2 to 4 inches above the soil line in order to maintain the dwarf effect. Eventually, the graft will heal into a small bump on the trunk of the tree.

2. If the hole is dug more than a few days after the tree is purchased or has arrived in the mail, the roots may be dry and need to be soaked in water for an hour. Some of the roots may be excessively long; it is acceptable to trim those to the same length as the others.

3. Position the tree. If you need an extra pair of hands but none are available, you may construct a tree support to lean the tree against while you are positioning the roots and filling in the hole around it. *For more information about making tree supports, see Chapter 4, under "Wood, hammer, and nails."* You will want to shovel in a

mound of dark organic soil on which to rest the roots while you spread them. If the roots have arrived in burlap, cut as much of it away as you can before re-filling the hole. Some may be trapped under the root ball, and that is fine because burlap will eventually decompose into the soil.

4.   Position the bottom branch down, toward the southwest to protect the tree from being damaged by the winter sun later in the year. If your garden is located on windy terrain, tipping the tree into the direction of the source of the wind about three to five degrees will help it withstand its force and the tree will eventually grow upright.

5.   Spread the roots out evenly across the expanse of the hole.

6.   Test the depth of the hole by placing the digging spade across it. If the top of the root crown is below the handle of the shovel, then the hole is deep enough.

7.   Shovel 3 inches of soil into the hole all around the outside of the root ball and pack it down firmly with the sole of your shoe or boot. Keep doing this until the soil in the hole is at the same level as the top of the root ball.

photo by Karen Szklany Gault

8.   Pile up a very short, firm wall of soil encircling the tree a foot from its trunk to capture the water you provide for it. This will keep the water close to the roots, which need it most

directly after it has been transplanted. The wall will eventually disappear.

Young trees need to be supported until they grow strong enough to withstand the elements on their own, particularly if they were planted with small root balls. Stakes are normally used for this purpose. Before you begin filling the hole, you may drive a stake into the ground, where it will reach 18 inches from the soil line when planting in heavy soil, and 24 inches in light soil. The best length for the stake that will be used with a tree of standard height is 7 ½ to 8 feet. Trees with big heads, such as the sweet cherry, will need the support of two stakes, spaced 18 inches apart and clearing the head by 2 to 3 inches. Those that are less than half the standard height would need a stake that is about 6 to 6 ½ feet.

photo by Karen Szklany Gault

If the roots have enough room to grow further, then it is time to start filling in the hole with soil. Organic soil created from worms or fully decomposed kitchen compost is best to fill in close to the roots as the bottom layer. This will encourage worms to gather underground at the level of the roots in order to create more nutrient-rich material to feed your tree. Bouncing the tree gently will help the soil settle around the roots before you begin filling in the hole with organic soil.

The process for adding organic material to your soil when planting is outlined below:

1. Above the layer of organic soil, place a layer of leaf, peat, or bark mulch, keeping it 18 inches away from the trunk to prevent the development of a fungal disease.

2. Place a layer of hay or straw on top of the mulch.

3. Apply a layer of topsoil. Pack the soil firmly with either your hands or the sole of your shoe.

4. When the hole is completely filled in, take out the short-term mechanical support that you built for it and press down on the soil with the sole of your shoe to set it firmly in place and to abolish any hidden air pockets.

5. Spread bark mulch around the surface, avoiding placement close to the trunk. This mulch both adds beauty to the landscape you are creating and feeds the soil with added nutrients.

6. If you secured a stake for the tree, it is time to tie the tree to it. If it is more than a year old, rubber tubing can be used with a figure eight pattern between the stake and the tree, using protective buffers to avoid chafing. Nurseries or gardening stores provide these.

Providing the tree with water is the final step of the planting process. You will want to create a short, raised soil ring around the rim of the hole with some of the soil, about two feet from the trunk, to retain water. This will catch the water you will provide for the tree, like a teacup saucer. Select a hose with a gentle flow of water and lay it on the ground near the base of the tree until the "saucer" fills, or place a sprinkler nearby in a position that will enable all the water to reach the expanse of the newly dug hole. Leave the hose or sprinkler in place until the soil around the tree is thoroughly soaked and settled. To keep the tree sufficiently irrigated, water the soil deeply once a week until the tree has been established.

PLANTING CITRUS FRUITS

The citrus tree family includes oranges, mandarins, tangerines, grapefruits, lemons, limes, and kumquats. Its scientific name is *Rutaceae*. These trees usually grow best in temperate climates, such as those in the Southeast region of the United States, Hawaii, Texas, the Southwestern states, and

Southern California. Southern California's Orange County is so named for a good reason. Bicycle riders are treated to miles of fragrant orange groves along residential side streets. Likewise, Florida is also well known for providing citrus fruits to the country year-round. Citrus fruits are a delicious source of vitamin C. Among the ways they are enjoyed include freshly squeezed for breakfast juices (orange and grapefruit) and cold summer drinks (lemonade and limeade), misted over salads,

photo by Matt Higgins

or cut into wedges. No matter how or when they are eaten, their flavor will wake you up.

Citrus fruit juice contains a high amount of acid, which comes from the soil in which this type of fruit is accustomed to growing. Knowledge about the type of soil you have to work with for growing your citrus trees is important, because this will determine how you enhance it to feed the trees with the proper nutrients vital to their growth and productivity. As you have learned, different types of soil contain different types of nutrients but need others added to adequately feed specific types of trees. Sandy soil needs help retaining water, which would be done by adding peat or seaweed. Soil made of adobe clay needs to be softened with compost. However, the soil may need to be prepared a season prior to planting if you need to add organic compost or mulch materials in order to support the trees you would like to grow. Adding them at the time of planting may make the tree more susceptible to fungal diseases.

If you are too short on time to grow a citrus tree from seeds or constructing your own tree graft, you may want to purchase a tree that has been propagated in a nursery and is ready to plant. This may significantly shorten the wait time before the tree begins to flower and bear fruit. It also ensures that the tree you will be growing will self-pollinate, as most citrus trees do, whether it is planted in the ground or grown in a pot on your patio. But, if you would still like to grow your trees from seeds, you would need to arrange for cross-pollination or hand-pollination of the flowers.

If you are patient and would like to meet the challenge of beginning a citrus tree from seed, you will need to take the following steps:

1. Wash the seeds that you glean from the type of fruit you would like to grow.

2. Plant the seeds in a container of warm potting soil that is big enough to allow roots to form and grow, about ¼ to ½ of an inch deep.

3. Water the seed and soil thoroughly, and continue to provide ample moisture throughout the germination process.

4. Set the container on a sunny windowsill and within a week a seedling may be visible above the soil line.

5. Train the seedling into a single stem by pruning back additional branches within 8 inches of the soil.

Most citrus fruit varieties do not produce sufficiently if planted on their own root systems. They are often grafted, or budded, onto the rootstock of host trees that are better adapted to a particular soil environment. This is a detail to consider once the seedlings you have begun are at least a year old and have begun to produce buds that develop into flowers.

The site chosen to plant a citrus fruit tree needs to offer plenty of sunlight, and be at least 6 to 8 feet away from any building, driveway, or fence. If you have more than one tree to plant on the site, they should be at least 12 to 18 feet from one another. They grow large heads, and keeping their branches away from windows and wires will keep your house safer from damage in the event of a storm. It may also save you some of the extra time and energy needed for trimming the branches if these distance requirements are followed. If they are planted too close to each other, they could compete for root space, water, soil nutrients, and sunshine. Keeping the distance between them will give them all an opportunity to grow and produce abundantly. If you will be planting the trees directly in the ground, this should be done from autumn through late winter in the states that support them, so that they have a chance to become established in their new environment before the extremely high temperatures and dry heat of summer assail them.

When removing the citrus cultivar from the pot that it has been propagated in, wash off at least an inch of potting material from the root ball. This will give the roots a chance to make direct contact with the surrounding soil. If the roots cling to the pot, it may be necessary to cut some of them away, which will stimulate them to grow in the soil that will surround them when they are planted in the ground.

The method of planting is important to the survival of a citrus tree.

1. Clear an area of bare soil a minimum of 3 ft. in diameter. This will allow room for watering the soil around the tree deeply and will guard the tree from competition from other types of vegetation.

2. In the center of the circle, dig a hole to the same height as the root ball. This will ensure that the roots will be totally buried and will not be exposed above the soil line. They need to stay underground to collect all the nutrients in the soil to feed the tree. This will also protect them from exposure to the wind and sun.

3. Place the tree in the middle of the hole you have just created, refill the hole with soil halfway up the root ball, and water the roots and soil. If the soil is sandy, mix peat moss with it before using it to refill the hole.

4. The next step is to add an extra inch of soil on top of the level of the root ball so that it will be surrounded by the soil in which it will be growing and to keep it moist.

5. After you water what you have planted, fill in the rest of the hole with soil and pat it down firmly. This will ensure that the roots stay moist and that the soil patted close around them will keep them warm. It is important to not pack soil around the tree above the level of the root ball. Citrus trees are very susceptible to foot rot, especially at the site where a graft has been made. *Foot rot is a fungal disease that will be discussed in greater detail in Chapter 9.*

6. With the surrounding soil, create a ring around the tree, raised ½ foot high, to hold water and keep it moist. Filling the ring with bark mulch will also help the soil around the tree retain the water that fills the ring.

The final step in the planting process of a citrus tree promotes the maintenance of proper irrigation. The tree will need to be watered in this way three times the first week after it has been planted. After this, it will need to be watered twice each week for the next three weeks. Soon after this, the ring you have built will begin to disappear. Once this happens, the tree is established and can be watered only as needed, with a sprinkler or a hose. Also, make sure that there is a surface area around the tree at least 3 feet in diameter that is kept free of weeds.

Once the tree has been established and new growth begins to appear, the application of lawn and turf fertilizer monthly through October will provide the tree with the micronutrients that it needs. There are specific citrus fertilizers also available both at garden centers and online. *You may also create them yourself, using the knowledge about soil that you gained in Chapter 3.*

PLANTING MELONS

Melons belong to the family of gourds called *Cucurbitaceae*, along with cucumbers and pumpkins. The sweet melon is named for the quality of its flavor, and its scientific name is *Cucumis melo*. There are several types

of sweet melons in this category: cantaloupe, honeydew, muskmelon, watermelon, and winter melon. Most varieties of melon are usually cut up and served as ingredients in fruit salads, formed into balls that float in party punches, dipped in yogurt as appetizers and snacks, or spooned out of their skins as a summer dessert. Their flavor is refreshing and their juice is an excellent source of water for your body throughout the hottest months of the year.

Melons grow on vines, close to the ground. They have seeds and depend on pollination for their production. Because they require warm soil to grow in, the proper method for planting melons depends on the climate in your region. If you live in a temperate zone, the weather patterns that you experience close to home are mild to moderate; there are no extremes of hot or cold weather. Under these conditions, you may sow melon seeds directly into the ground soil of your garden. If you live in a cooler climate, you will have to sow the seeds into a container and cultivate them on a sunny windowsill for a month before it is safe to transfer them to a cold frame in your garden until the soil temperature rises to at least 64 degrees. At that time it will be safe to plant them directly into the ground soil that you have prepared for them.

Cold frames are wooden or plastic planting frames used for young plants that need extra protection from low ground temperatures when they are planted early in the growing season. They are used to assist plants that normally grow in warmer temperature ranges to adapt to the ground soil temperature in cooler climates, gradually. They are very similar in appearance to raised beds, but they have an added feature. A cover of glass or a frame of plastic that looks like a miniature greenhouse or tent is placed over them to capture the warmth of the sun. They are kept outside to foster the plants' acclimation to your garden's climate patterns. This step increases their chance of survival and growth once they are planted directly into the ground.

If you are among the home gardeners who live in a less temperate climate, you will need to find some containers in which to sow your melon seeds and keep them in a pot or box.

1.   Sow the seeds ½ inch deep in soil and moisten the soil thoroughly.

2.   Place a glass or plastic top on the pot or box and let them germinate on a sunny windowsill. You could also set up a table for your seedlings with special plant lights.

3.   The temperature of the room you keep them in should be sufficiently warm (64 to 70 degrees Fahrenheit).

It is important to prepare the soil for planting your melons at least one month ahead of time. If you plan to plant your melon seedlings in late May, you will need to begin about four weeks before that to turn a layer of well-rotted compost or manure into the soil. Then do the same again two weeks before planting. After the second round, water the soil well and place polythene plastic over the soil, which is kept in position by short stakes, to warm it. The word polythene is a shortened version of polyethylene, a type of thin, flexible plastic.

When the seedlings have produced at least three leaves, it is time to plant them in the ground outdoors.

1. Using a trowel, dig a hole in the soil twice the size of the root ball, to leave them room to grow. As a precaution against the plants developing soft rot, keep half the soil ball formed around the roots above the soil line.

2. Water the roots and soil gently, avoiding the stem.

3. Dig holes for each of the seedlings, leaving 3 to 4 feet between each of them.

4. For 7 to 10 days, keep the plants in their cold frames, shaded if they are located in an area exposed to direct sunlight.

5. Once the fifth leaf appears on each of the plants, pinch the stem to encourage more side shoots to grow.

6. A few weeks later, take the strongest of all the plants and train them in a separate frame by placing four of them in each of the four corners of the frame and stretching out their leafy branches toward one another.

7. Water them gently but thoroughly, always avoiding the stems.

After the plants have been established, shading may be gradually decreased. In the summer, this encourages pollination by the bees once the plants have begun flowering. Some hand pollination might also be needed to encourage the plants to flower and bear fruit their first season.

PLANTING BRAMBLES

The scientific name for the bramble family is *Rubus*. Blackberry, raspberry, and dewberry plants are categorized as brambles, which have branches that take the form of thorny canes growing in clusters. These canes take a variety of shapes: upright stems, arched stems, vines that grow horizontally and close to the ground, and vines that cling to either one another or a garden feature onto which they are trained. They may also be trained around structures such as

photo by Lucia Papile

fences, gates, arbors, columns, posts, or statues. Pergolas and trellises are the most common features used for that purpose. Brambles used to be known for their thorns, but there are now varieties that have been created without the thorns, a new attribute that occasionally compromises their hardiness. Roger Swain, the former host of PBS' *Victory Gardens*, recommends the Chester blackberry variety as the hardiest of the thornless blackberries. Brambles are considered weeds by some, but the fruit they produce is delicious. The berries are often baked in cobblers or turned into jams to spread in blintzes or on toast. They have also been whipped into fools (a type of pudding that includes egg whites) and fermented for wine. Sometimes they are eaten with a dollop of cream for an afternoon tea, or as a layer in a parfait with yogurt and granola.

Steps to take before planting

Before beginning the planting process, it is important to note that the root systems of brambles are perennial, which means they produce canes every year, but they produce fruit biennially, or every other year. The initial non-fruiting canes are called primocanes. Those that produce flowers and fruit are called floricanes. These canes die right after their fruiting season, but as this happens, the roots begin growing the primocanes for the following "vegetative" season, as the non-fruiting season is called by horticulturists. For example, if your raspberry canes bear fruit in 2010, that is their fruiting, or floricane, season. In 2011 the plant will grow only primocanes, and that summer will be considered its vegetative season. The following season, the summer of 2012, will again be a fruiting season. If cared for well, brambles will live and produce fruit for as long as ten years.

Selecting a site for planting your brambles requires careful consideration of the prevailing climate conditions. They are best protected from strong, dry winds, but planting a row of hedges near the location where the brambles will grow could solve this. The air circulation that a gentle breeze provides will protect the roots from developing a fungal disease. If you keep the soil that the brambles are planted in moist, without subjecting the roots to saturation by standing water, you will help prevent the development of fungal diseases. Regions with especially humid summers might contribute to this risk. This might be why they grow best in the cooler northern states of the country, particularly where there are mountains and boreal forests.

Preparing the soil for planting brambles will ensure a long and productive life for your plants. Brambles grow in soil that is slightly more acidic (pH of 5.8 to 6.2). They thrive best in soil that is at least three percent organic, usually a mix of sand and loam that is prepared a year ahead of planting and kept moist. This mixture is meant to suppress weed growth, but weeding may need to be done on a regular basis to keep the growing bramble roots free of unwanted detritus. It is also important to grow your brambles in soil that has not previously supported tomatoes, potatoes, melon, eggplant, or strawberries, which may carry viruses that would kill your young plants. Be very cautious of wild brambles that already grow in close proximity to your garden. They can also carry diseases that would kill your domestically propagated plants. Finally, if you plan to turn over soil on which grass has been growing, it is important to check closely whether or not white grubs or wireworms are present. *These pests will be discussed in Chapter 8.* If you do detect their presence, it may be better to grow pumpkins or sweet corn on the site of your future berries for a couple of years to purge the soil.

Discerning the best brambleberry to grow

Not only will you need to take into consideration the special needs of brambles when choosing where to plant them, you will also need to know which varieties thrive best in your temperature zone. Blackberries tolerate deeper drops in temperature than raspberries and remain firmer when they are ripe. They also tolerate higher amounts of humidity without becoming more susceptible to fungal diseases. If you have a preference for canes that are thornless, your choice of plants will be more limited. Ultimately, the best choice is the berry that is most appealing to your palate. If you are unsure of which you would enjoy best, you could visit several farms around your home that grow different brambleberry varieties and allow you to pick a pint of your own. This would give you the chance to sample several and make an informed decision.

If you have received dormant, catalog-ordered, bare-rooted, or pot-grown bramble cultivars in the mail, you will want to keep them warm and moist by planting them in the ground as early in the spring as the ground is soft enough to provide a measure of workability. At this time in the season, the air is still cool and not very humid. Choosing a cloudy, windless day in early spring will ensure that the roots will not be exposed to more sunlight or wind than they can withstand. Many blackberry varieties, especially the trailing and semi-erect, have roots that are especially light sensitive. They may not survive the transplant if their roots are exposed to direct sunlight at the time of planting. They need a chance to establish themselves in the garden before they are exposed to the elements. Beyond that point, plenty of water and sunshine will help them grow and produce an abundance of berries.

Preparing to transplant brambles

Brambles are grown in rows and placed in the garden where they can stay for at least ten years. When digging rows of holes for planting them, it is important to leave room for movement around them. Keep in mind that you need to fertilize often with a hand tiller and stand close to the plant in order to harvest the berries. The chart below reflects the spacing requirements for a variety of brambles.

Spacing of Bramble Plants

Berry Type	Spacing of Rows	Spacing Along the Row
Raspberries - general	6-12 feet apart	2-3 feet apart
Raspberries - fruiting/ floricane	8-12 feet apart	9-15 inches apart
Blackberries - general	10-12 feet apart	2-4 feet apart
Blackberries - trailing	10-12 feet apart	5-6 feet apart
Dewberries	8-10 feet apart	3-4 feet apart

Digging the holes for brambles

The holes dug for brambles should be wide enough to allow the roots to be spread out and to grow further.

1. Raspberries that are planted bare-rooted should be planted in the ground an inch deeper than they grew in the nursery. This will offer greater protection from temperature extremes.

2. Blackberries should be planted at the same depth at which they grew in the nursery. If this information is not written out or offered, you will want to ask the nursery staff for such details.

3. Plants that have been tissue-cultured should be planted with the soil plug that they were purchased with, and the hole that they will be transplanted into dug at the same depth of the plug. Tissue-cultured plants are propagated with live, growing plant tissue and are transplanted while they are actively growing instead of dormant. A soil plug is the soil surrounding the roots of a plant that has been cultivated for transplanting.

4. Nursery-mature, tissue-cultured plants are usually purchased while they are dormant and may not have a soil plug. They should be pruned down to ground level before transplanting. Nursery-mature plants have grown in the ground for a few months at a nursery in order to acclimate them for growth in an outside garden, and to prepare them for the rigors of transplanting. As a result of the pruning described above, the root system below the earth is not burdened with the support of many leaves while it is still very young. Instead, the branches and leaves grow and mature at the same pace as the roots. This process also prevents the spread of any disease that may be present on the canes that have already grown before transplantation.

Completing the planting process

The final step of the planting process is to refill the hole with soil and pack it down firmly with either your hands or the sole of your shoe. Next, water the soil around the roots of the planted brambles. If your region receives less than one inch of rainfall per week, water needs to be trickled into the soil to keep it moist. Raspberries also need to be fed a generous amount of potassium and nitrogen, which may be applied to the soil with mulch materials, such as dried leaves. If organic mulch materials are not very accessible to you, application of a nitrogen-rich organic fertilizer will give your brambles what they need. Topping the soil with a layer of straw will help hold in the moisture and enhance the nutrients in the mulch or fertilizer. This extra care will help your brambles produce an abundant berry harvest.

PLANTING BUSH BERRIES

Berry plants that are considered members of the bush family are blueberries, bilberries, cranberries, currants, gooseberries, jostaberries, and lingonber-

ries. These plants are grown as much for their beauty as for the berries they produce. The flowers that bloom on them are shaped like bells and their leaves provide colorful foliage in autumn. The berries that they grow are very small and they require a cool, dark, moist soil for growing that is very acidic. The acidity of their soil affects their flavor, because most of them are tart, sour, or bitter-sweet.

Blueberries range in color from dark blue to black and are closely related to huckleberries. Although the two are often referred to interchangeably, huckleberries are reported to be slightly sweeter. On the other hand, the sweetness of blueberries is more subdued. Both types of berries are often eaten mixed into pancakes or oatmeal, baked in muffins, pressed into jams, or fermented to produce wine. Cranberries are sweet and bright red. They are enjoyed in a wide variety of forms, such as fruit juices, margarita mixes, tarts, pies, cakes, scones, breads, mousses, compotes, dried and tossed with salads, diced into salsas, and baked as a garnish on poultry. Lingonberries are also bright red, like cranberries, but they are a little plumper. Their flavor is tart, so they are sweetened and eaten in the form of jams, compotes, juices, and syrups. Gooseberries are usually bright orange, but others are purple or deep green. They may also grow in a variety of other colors, as well. They are most often baked into tarts and pies because they have a sour flavor and rest best on the tongue when mixed with sugar. Currants are white, red, pink, or black. Black currants are close to purple in color. They also have a sour taste, but one that is tempered, and closer to a grape in its earthiness than a gooseberry. Juices and wines are made from them. The jostaberry is a cross between gooseberry and black currant, and has a similar flavor. Likewise, currants, gooseberries, and jostaberries are often used to make pies and jellies. The quality that all of these berries possess in common is that they are small and soft, and their flowers are usually self-pollinating. This allows them to produce tiny seeds that are barely noticeable and can be eaten along with the fruit. Their scientific family name is *Ribes*.

Blueberries

The scientific name for the plant family that includes blueberries is *Ericaceae*. Blueberries grow better at higher elevations, so if there is a hill in your garden to plant your blueberry bushes on, they will reward you with a plethora of plump, sweet berries. Blueberries are one of the few fruits that are native to North America, but only grow wild in the Pacific Northwest. The rest of the country must purchase and plant them in their gardens. The most common types of blueberries are named the lowbush, halfhigh, highbush, and rabbiteye. Different varieties perform better in different regions of the continent.

photo by Herb Stanfield

The Northeastern states and Eastern Canada are the best places to grow lowbush blueberry varieties, which do not grow very tall and have branches that keep close to the ground. Their scientific name is *Vaccinium angustifolium* and they produce fruit every other year. The halfhigh blueberry bush, a hybrid of the lowbush and highbush varieties, but listed with the highbush variety under the scientific name *Vaccinium corymbosum*, has been cultivated to withstand harsher climates that offer more temperature extremes than their parent varieties, while still producing an abundant crop of berries. Blueberry farmers in Minnesota and Wisconsin have grown halfhigh blueberries successfully after other varieties have not thrived in that region. On the other hand, the classic highbush varieties, *Vaccinium corymbosum*, are the type most often grown in home gardens. They thrive better in states located from the Mid-Atlantic coastline and Central states to the Midwest, as well as the Pacific Northwest.

Although they are a variation of the highbush varieties, rabbiteye varieties are the type best suited to southern climates. They require a less acidic soil and are more resistant to pests and diseases. Wild rabbiteye bushes may grow as high as thirty feet tall. Those cultivated for home gardens range from 5 to 20 feet tall. On the other hand, they are being grown less often than the low-chill highbush varieties because they produce smaller, seedier berries and require cross-pollination. The low-chill highbush varieties produce well as far south as central Florida because they are cultivated to require less time at temperatures below 45 degrees Fahrenheit. They ripen in late April or early May, ahead of most of the other varieties.

In general, most blueberry varieties grow best in sunny areas that host a growing season of at least five months. They have long, hair-like roots that can extend as far as 32 inches deep, and the highbush varieties may grow as big as 8 feet tall. They produce best if they spend between 600 and 1,000 hours, at temperatures below 45 degrees Fahrenheit and are suited to slightly more acidic soil. The pH range most conducive to high productivity for blueberries is 3.8 to 5.2, with the optimum range at 4.5 to 4.8. Sandy, loam soils fall into this category. Blueberries also need their soil to be full of organic matter. Sowing buckwheat and oat cover crops the autumn before you plan to start growing your blueberries will aid their acclimation when they are transplanted. Accordingly, materials such as compost, leaves, and peat moss are best used as organic supplements to the soil.

Whether you purchase your blueberry plants directly from a nursery or mail order them, you will most likely bring home a plant that is either bare-rooted or has a soil plug due to being cultivated in a container. Plants purchased when they are two or three years old have the most chance of survival and productivity. If you purchase a bare-rooted plant, make sure that it is dormant when you plant it. If a container-grown plant is purchased several weeks before the intended planting date, it may be kept outside and watered as needed.

Make sure that the site chosen for planting your blueberries receives full sun exposure. Within that requirement, there are several options for the layout of your blueberry bush collection. They may be planted individually around your lawn as a landscaping feature or in a cluster. If added to a garden that will be used for growing other types of fruits or berries, they are often planted in rows. It is beneficial to have at least two in close proximity to one another to ensure cross-pollination. This will give them a chance to produce bigger berries and produce more prolifically. The spacing of the plants also depends on the variety. In general, the space between rows ranges between 8 to 12 feet, depending on what type of garden equipment you will be using for the ongoing care of the plants. The specific spacing requirements within each row for the different varieties are reflected in the chart provided below.

Blueberry variety	Space Between Bushes
Highbush	4-5 feet
Halfhigh	2 ½ to 3 feet
Lowbush	1 foot
Rabbiteye	8 feet
Dewberries	8-10 feet apart

Several days before planting blueberries, it is best to soak a bale of peat for use in and around the hole you will be digging. It is difficult to keep wet, but if it is prepared by soaking, it will hold the moisture in the soil around the plants. When digging the hole, it is important to remember that a larger diameter is more important than depth. Because the root systems of blueberry plants are thick and shallow, the soil line should be as high as the plant was grown in at the nursery. The nursery staff will be able to give you this information. The space in the hole should be wide enough to spread the roots out completely, with room for them to grow further. To plant your blueberries, follow these steps after digging your hole:

1. Place 5 to 6 gallons of soaking wet peat in the hole.

2. Mix with the same amount of soil to create a 50/50 combination.

3. Create a mound of soil for the plant to rest on.

4. Spread out the roots to their full length.

5. Fill the rest of the hole with the dirt that was dug from it originally.

6. Pay close attention to the soil line on the branches and match that.

7. Pat the soil down firmly with your hands or the sole of your shoes.

8. Water well.

Keep in mind that if you plan to support your blueberry bush with stakes, you will need them to be about 3½ to 4 inches in height. Once the hole has been filled in with soil, the stakes may be tied to the tree with pieces of a cotton rag or another light material that would not bite into the trunk.

When all your blueberry bushes have been planted, it is possible to inoculate them against an unwanted fungal disease by encouraging beneficial fungi to grow around them. One way to do this is to take the soil and leaf mulch from the base of wild blueberry plants and scatter them around the base of your newly planted bushes.

Other bush berries

Cranberries, lingonberries, whortleberries, and bilberries belong to the same plant family as blueberries and also require acidic soil to grow. Lingonberries grow to a height of about 12 to 18 inches, and their branches spread out to about 18 inches in length. The lingonberry bush grows low and far. They

thrive best in cooler climates, making them a good choice for growers who live in New England, Southeast Alaska, and the Pacific Northwest. The scientific name for lingonberry is *Vaccinium vitis-idaea.* Likewise, cranberries also grow very abundantly in bogs throughout New England. Their scientific name is *Vaccinium oxycoccos.*

photo by Edward S. Gault

Lingonberries do not grow well in extreme temperatures, either cold or hot. In northern climates, it is best to give them full sun exposure for optimal productivity. They will need some protection from high winds or they might suffer damage. In warmer climates that are subject to extremes of heat and drought, planting them in partial shade can offer them relief and help them thrive. It is best to plant them in acidic soil with a pH between 5.0 and 5.8, with a wide clearing that is free of weeds. The soil must drain well and contain around 2 percent of organic matter. Including moist peat moss in the planting process will most likely benefit their health, because it increases the level of acidity in the soil and aids the retention of moisture.

When planting lingonberries:

1. Dig a hole with a depth that matches the depth of the soil in which it was potted.

2. The hole needs to be dug large enough in diameter to allow the roots plenty of room to spread and grow.

3. Place the plant in the hole and spread out the roots.

4. Pack the soil firmly around them with the sole of your shoe, so that it is settled there when the remainder of the hole is filled in.

5. Leave a distance of 18 inches free around the lingonberry plant on all sides.

When planning the number of berry plants to grow, it is important to remember the height and breadth that the plant is expected to attain when mature. If you know the measurements of the space in your garden where you plan to grow them, you will know how many you will be able to plant there. The following chart provides the height and breadth requirements of most bush berries in the *Ribes* family, when planted in a row. Anywhere from about 8 to 12 feet should be left between rows of all these berry bushes. Giving them this space allows them the room to grow and the room for you to prune and harvest.

Berry	Height	Breadth
Lingonberry	12-18 inches	18 inches
Red and White Currant - row - hedge	3-5 feet	3-5 feet 2 to 2 ½ at right angle
Black Currant	5 feet	5 feet
Gooseberry	2-5 feet	2-5 feet
Jostaberries	6-8 feet	6-8 feet

These small berry plants, such as the gooseberry and currant, are different from most others because the best time to plant them is the fall. The bush begins to form leaves and grow early the following spring. If planted in the fall, the roots will become better established and stronger shoots will grow when the ground thaws. When planting a young berry bush, the size of the hole in which it should be planted is best measured by a bushel basket for its diameter and depth.

If you are planting an older small-berry-bush:

1. Plant it so that the soil covers the bottom two or three buds.

2. As with other bush berries, the soil around the roots should be made firm with the sole of your shoe before the rest of the hole is filled in.

3. Water the ground thoroughly.

4. Place a layer of mulch that is several inches thick around the base of the plant, which will help absorb excess moisture and suppress the growth of weeds.

PLANTING STRAWBERRIES

Strawberries have been classified in the bush berry family, but the plant that produces them also belongs to the rose family. They are listed separately in this guide because they have unique propagation, planting, and growing requirements.

The scientific name for the plant family that includes strawberries is *Fragaria*. The species of strawberries cultivated in the United States have resulted from the interbreeding of several regional species. The main parent species that have been used for this interbreeding are the English, *F. vesca*; North American, *F. virginiana*; and the South American, *F. chiloensis*. The cultivar offspring of those parents can be grouped into four types:

1. The summer-fruiting strawberry yields only one crop of berries early in the summer. A crop is the yield of fruit produced by a plant. Those that yield a crop in both the summer and the fall are called two-crop cultivars.

2. The perpetual strawberry keeps re-fruiting in erratic bursts until the first frost. As a result of this fruiting pattern, they are referred to as "ever-bearing."

3. The day-neutral variety tolerates more shade than the others do, and is also considered an ever-bearing plant.

4. The alpine strawberry is a type of wild mountain strawberry. It is a subspecies of *F. vesca*, named *F. alpina*. They produce bunches of white flowers and dark red fruit, and yield crops in "flushes" from June through November. A flush is a burst of fruit flowering and production that happens more than once in a season. There are usually periods between each burst when no flower or fruit forms on the plant.

All types of strawberry plants are cultivated in the same fashion and are expected to yield a total of 8 to 10 ounces per bush. This amount is equal to a half-pint carton full of plump strawberries, similar to those sold on a farm. It is also comparable to a small plastic container of strawberries at the grocery store. Multiply that amount by the number of bushes you will plant, and that will give you an estimate of the crop size you could anticipate from your strawberry patch.

Sunlight

Keep in mind that strawberry plants categorized as ever-bearing need more hours of sunlight to produce an abundant yield. The recommendation is between 6 and 10 hours for an abundant crop. The only exception to this is the day-neutral strawberry, which is more tolerant of shade. When purchasing your strawberry cultivars, you may want to consult with the nursery staff about the sunlight requirements of the different varieties that they offer in order to determine which will work best in your garden. They may also be able to give you guidance about which plants are the most disease-resistant.

Soil

The soil where strawberries are grown needs to be well drained and slightly acidic (6.0 to 6.5 pH). Soil that retains water may cause the roots to become waterlogged, which makes them more vulnerable to soil-borne pests and diseases. Most soils can be enhanced with organic material to make the ground amenable to growing strawberries. It is important to change their location every three or four years, which gives the soil a rest from the drain on nutrients that strawberry plants cause. The soil will need to be re-worked and enhanced with more organic materials, then planted with disease-resistant vegetables, such as pumpkins. Planting them closer to vegetables than your other fruits will give those fruits less competition for the water and nutrients in the soil, and a chance to also produce an abundant crop. *By doing this, you will protect your other fruit and berry plants from the same threats that strawberry bushes are susceptible to, which will be discussed in greater detail in Chapter 8.* The vegetables grow best in soil that drains water well, which will also benefit your strawberries. Likewise, planting them at a higher elevation can help quicken the pace of water drainage and provide more hours of direct sunlight. However, make sure they are planted on a different hill than the blueberries, which also produce well at slightly higher elevations.

Runner production and spacing

All strawberries are self-pollinating, so this detail does not enter the equation when planning their placement in your garden. The important aspect to keep in mind is which plants produce runners and which do not. This will give you an idea where to dig the holes. A runner is the offshoot a "parent" plant is expected to create, from which future cultivars are taken, and from which future fruit crops are expected to grow.

There are three basic systems for spacing strawberry plants in your garden: the matted-row system, the spaced-matted-row system, and the hill system. The choice of which type to use will depend upon the amount of runners a strawberry plant is expected to produce. The matted-row system is the simplest and requires the least labor of the three methods. It would be used for the June-bearing plants, because they produce the most runners. The plants are spaced 18 to 24 inches apart within each row, and 3 to 4 feet between rows. The "mother" plants are allowed to set as many runners as they can produce, which are spread out to extend the length of space provided between plants, both within each row and between rows.

The same initial amount of space is given between plants in the spaced-matted-row system, but only a certain amount of runners are allowed to establish themselves in the soil to become new fruiting plants. They are spread out and kept in place by a U-shaped wire that looks like a hairpin. The rest of the runners are removed. This process is more labor-intensive, but it increases the yield of the plants because they are pruned and given more room for fruit to grow. As a result, they are competing less against each other for the nutrients in the soil. It also allows more air to circulate between them, and therefore reduces the risk of the plant developing a fungal disease.

Finally, the hill system is usually used for plants that produce fewer runners, such as the "ever-bearing" and "day-neutral" varieties. The plants are placed about 12 inches apart and staggered in double rows. All runners are removed from the parent plant and not allowed to propagate, which eventually decreases the yield of the plants. It is generally used when working from raised beds instead of when planting directly in the ground. The Alpine strawberry could thrive when planted in the hill system, because it does not generally produce runners and is usually cultivated from seeds.

Planting

The planting season for strawberries differs according to the U.S. region in which they are being grown. For the Northeast, Northwest, Northern California, Alaska, the Mountain states, and Great Lakes regions, the planting season is April to early May. For the Mid-Atlantic, Central, and Plains states, the months to plant strawberries are March and April. In Southern climates, they can be planted as early as February.

When the plants arrive, they are likely to be bare-rooted. They must not be stored in the same place as ripening fruit because the ethylene gas from the fruit could damage them. To prevent their drying out, it is important to moisten the roots, wrap them in burlap, and place a plastic bag around the burlap. To prevent the growth of a fungal disease, make sure they do not become soggy. When you are ready to plant them in the ground, keep several cultivars of the same variety in a tub of water, covered in a cloth to keep them moist while you work the soil and dig their holes. The moisture and cloth covering protect them from strong winds and direct sunlight, two elemental extremes that they are too fragile to withstand exposure to. To reap the best results from your strawberry plants, place them in the soil on a day that is cloudy and cool, but not windy. This adds extra protection from the stress of extreme weather conditions during the planting process.

In order to work the ground properly and make the soil amenable to growing strawberry plants, the best tools to use when planting your cultivars are a hand trowel and fork.

1. The ground needs to be thoroughly weeded with the fork before the planting begins.

2. Use the fork to loosen the soil before digging the hole for the plant.

3. Use the trowel to make a hole that is deep enough to cover the roots up to the crown, which is the area between the roots and the stem. The hole should also be wide enough to spread out the roots to their full length and give them room to grow further. If it is planted too deep, the lowest buds may

photo by Karen Szklany Gault

   rot, but, if planted in too shallow a hole, the roots may not receive enough water to become established.

4. Remove all the runners and leaves, and cut off dried-out roots.

5. Place the plant in the hole and spread out the roots in all directions.

6. Surround the roots with soil and refill the rest of the hole, up to the roots' crown at the bottom of the stem.

7. Pack the soil firmly around the roots with your hands.

8. Give each plant about 2 cups of water with a sprinkler, watering wand, or a watering can. They all provide a way to water the plants gently.

9. Once the plants have settled, check the depth of the soil around the plant one more time to determine that it does not need adjustment.

10. The final step in the process of planting strawberries is to shovel a two-inch layer of straw mulch around the plants to keep the soil moist and cool and to increase the nutritional quality of the soil.

For the first few weeks after planting, it is important to water the strawberry bushes regularly, but to keep the ground free from soaking so that the forming fruit may be kept dry. Watering is best done in the morning, which will give enough time for the water to evaporate during the day, and reduce the risk that the fruit will be subject to mold that may form if the soil is left too moist overnight.

If you have been growing a variety that does not produce runners, such as the alpine strawberry, you will have to propagate a new plant by dividing the root system of an established plant in half by September, while the roots are still actively growing and will more easily replace the roots that have been split off. The next step is to plant each half in a separate pot, using the soil line on the stem as a guide to the depth at which to plant them in their new soil environment. However, Alpine strawberry varieties are generally grown from seeds sown in the fall. These seedlings are raised in cold frames over the winter months.

The other time to grow strawberries is in March.

1. Strawberry seeds are sown into seed boxes in moist soil with compost added.

2. Cover the potted seeds with glass, and keep them shaded at a temperature range of 64 to 68 degrees Fahrenheit.

3. Sufficient germination involves the production of two leaves on the stem of a seedling. Once this has happened, prick the buds of each seedling and place them into a box or a pot full of peat.

4. In May, when the danger of frost is over, plant the seedlings in the ground 1 foot apart, with 2 ½ feet between the rows.

PLANTING GRAPE VINES

Grapes belong to the botanical family called *Vitis*. Many of the grapes grown in American gardens today are bunch grapes with European origin. This means that they grow in clusters, or bunches, on the stem. The mus-

cadine varieties are the only types of grape that do not grow in bunches on the stem. Instead, they grow as individual berries. They are unique in another way, as well — their origins can be traced to the colonial period of the United States. However, all types of grapes grow on vines and are usually harvested abundantly in late October. None of the varieties thrive well in extreme temperatures, such as those found in the arctic or equatorial regions, but they will grow and produce quality fruit as far north as New England. The deep purple, fragrant concord grape *(Vitis lambrusca)* was first developed as a subspecies in Concord, Massachusetts. It is the one grape that contains seeds that are hard to separate from the edible pulp, but their sweet flavor makes it well worth the endeavor. It is a type of bunch grape that has a long history (almost 200 years) of successful cultivation in home gardens. Their trellis-borne leafy vines offer beautiful ornamentation, in addition to the sweet fragrance and flavor of their fruit.

The muscadine grape varieties grow best in the Southeastern pocket of the United States, where the Atlantic Ocean meets the Gulf of Mexico. That is the region of the country where their origin lies. The South Central states of Mississippi, Louisiana, and Alabama also have climates that are friendly to muscadine grapes along their Gulf coastline. Muscadines require regular rainfall, so they would not grow well in the desert climates of the Midwest and Southwest. They do not tolerate temperatures below 0 degrees Fahrenheit and require a frost-free growing period of at least 200 days, while most of the other varieties require a growing season that lasts between 160 and 180 days. Although most muscadine varieties are purple to black in color and offer an earthy flavor, the Scuppernong that is native to North Carolina is golden in color and the sweetest member of the family. Because a wide range of variance exists regarding the best fit between grape species and climate, it is best to consult the nursery staff where you buy your cultivars for recommendations about which varieties would grow best in your garden.

Location

Planting most bunch grapes at higher elevations than other fruits will protect them from damage that may occur from a low-lying frost pocket. It is important to note that grape vines do not enter a period of complete dormancy due to their low-temperature tolerance. They often keep growing through the colder months. Planting them parallel to the prevailing wind direction will prevent elemental damage and increase the air circulation around them. Attention to the amount of direct sunlight that your garden receives daily will determine the direction that the vines should be planted in the rows set aside for them. A north-to-south direction, on a south-facing slope, allows the vines to use the direct sunlight to its best advantage, benefitting the sugar development and the rate of ripening of the fruit.

Preparing the soil

Very little soil preparation is necessary before planting grape vines. A pH range from 6.0 to 7.5 (neutral) is sufficient for them, with the most common being 6.5. Sandy loam and slightly gravelly soils work best as their growing environment. Only 5 percent of the soil content should be made of organic compost material. Too much will cause the vines to become too leafy and to produce fewer or smaller fruit that ripens late. Enough compost to enable the soil to retain water without becoming drenched is sufficient. It is necessary to avoid standing water conditions in the soil that supports grape vines, particularly because of their susceptibility to fungal diseases.

Planting the grape vines

American bunch grape varieties are propagated most often from cuttings that are allowed to root directly from the stem to the soil. Those of European origin are sold as scions grafted onto the rootstock of American vines that are resistant to the grape phylloxera, a pest in the louse family. *This will be discussed in greater detail in Chapter 8.* Muscadines are bought when they are a year old and planted in the ground in layers. The vines should be at least one centimeter wide.

The more tolerant of the cold a grapevine variety is, the earlier it may be planted in spring. In the northern regions, this would be late April to early May. In warmer states, planting them in early autumn or winter will not hurt them. Southern California and the Southeastern states are warm enough to allow planting from December through February, if the vines are dormant. If the garden is not ready for the vine stock when it arrives, the roots may be moistened, covered, and kept in a container at 36 degrees Fahrenheit for a day or so. Or it may be heeled-in until the ground is ready for planting. Heeling-in means that a plant is temporarily laid at an angle and the roots buried to hold it until it is planted in the ground. This can be done with the plant still in the pot. When it is time to plant the vines, cut back only dried or dead roots and soak them for only an hour or two. This will make the soil around the roots clump together, which will give the roots extra protection from temperature drops in the spring.

When it is time to plant the vines, follow these instructions:

1. Dig furrows ten to 12 inches long, enough to spread the roots out and leave room for growth. None of the healthy roots should be cut back to the size of smaller ones.

2. The furrows should be dug longer to accommodate the longest roots. These roots carry the carbohydrates necessary to the development of the young vines. Cutting them would damage the potential growth and productivity of the vine. The depth of the furrows should match those the vines were cultivated in at the nursery.

3. Make sure that the top roots are at least 3 inches below the level of the soil. For grafted vines, the site of the graft union needs to be

above the level of the soil once it has been patted firm around the root system.

The distance required between each grape vine depends on the volume of growth expected of the individual vine, and this great variance is unique to growing grapes. Those that do not grow very vigorously may be planted as close as 3 feet apart, but those that do grow vigorously may require up to 6 feet between them. Muscadines are very vigorous growers and often require up to 20 feet between each plant in a row. The space between rows also depends on how large an area of the garden is designated for growing grapes. A small, homegrown vineyard usually needs only 9 feet between them, and this is also acceptable for muscadines. Once the vines are planted, they need to be watered well so that an air pocket does not dry out the roots.

Trellis design

Deeply rooted in the process of growing grapevines is the artful presentation of the vines and fruit. Different types of structures are used for this purpose, but the trellis has been the one most closely associated with grapevine growing. A trellis is a frame for grapevines to wrap around as they are growing. It may be made of latticed wood or of wire and poles. Its main purpose is to support the growth of the vines and the production of fruit. Supporting the vines to keep them and their fruit off the ground is important to their health and vigor. If it is ornate, the trellis may also serve as a garden ornament. The leafy canopy that forms overhead will be a welcome patch of fragrant shade in the middle of a summer day.

Part of the beauty of the trellis is its versatility. It can take a variety of shapes, from simple to ornate. There are a number of options for trellis designs that can be used if you wish to keep a small vineyard as part of your edible garden. Each will require a different pattern of pruning and training of the vines. The type of vine support most commonly used by home gardeners is an arbor, a short, latticed trellis for supporting vines. If more than one row of grapevines is planned, a trellis of greater size and complexity will be necessary.

Building the trellis

The basic materials that you will need for creating a trellis of wire and posts include end posts, line posts, and heavy wire. All materials need to be sturdy enough to support grapevines that are heavily laden with fruit.

Basic trellis construction is built on a fundamental design framework:

1. End posts are the first component put into place. The end posts are the piece of the trellis that is under the most tension, because they contain the place from which the wires may be tightened when necessary. These need to be well anchored into the ground at a depth of between 3 and 4 feet, leaning away from the rest of the trellis at a 30-degree angle. A minimum height of 9 feet and diameter of 5 inches will give the end poles enough volume to hold the weight of the wires and grape-heavy vines at peak fruit production. Used utility posts have been recycled for this purpose, but cedar posts that have been rendered non-toxically resistant to rot are an alternative.

2. Line posts are the next piece of the trellis to anchor into the ground at a full perpendicular angle to the ground, and at a depth of 2 to 2 ½ feet. The minimum height for these posts is between 8 and 9 feet, and 3 inches in diameter. Traditionally, these posts have been made of wood, but more modern versions are metal. The metal posts may be easier to handle, but they bend more easily when the vines grow heavy with fruit. Using a

mix of wood and metal posts may be easier on your back than using all wood. Spacing between them varies between 20 and 24 feet, depending on the system you decide to use for training the vines. If they are spaced more than 24 feet apart, the wires will sag. The most common spacing for a trellis system is three vines at eight feet apart between two posts at 24 feet apart. The wires support the cordons that extend directly from the trunk. A cordon is an extension of the trunk of a grape vine, which usually grows horizontally. From a cordon are usually born arms, canes, or shoots, which are the various types of growth that bring forth flowers and fruit. The trunk is the stem of a grapevine that grows vertically above the ground. An individual vine may grow more than one trunk.

3. Wire that supports the vine cordons is produced in different gauges of thickness. Lower gauge numbers indicate thicker wires. The top wire needs to be the thickest, and therefore a gauge of 9 is the minimum to use for that one. A gauge of 10 or 11 is sufficient for the bottom wires. Galvanized wire is gentler on the vines and lasts longer. The simplest trellis for a home gardener to build is one with three wires. The minimum distance between the top wire and the ground should be about 5 ½ to 6 feet, and 2 ½ to 3 feet for the lowest. The middle wire is placed at an equal distance between the top and bottom wires. Fasten the wires to the end posts by wrapping them around the post two times, then twisting the end of the wire back and around itself three times.

4. Fence staples are used to fasten the wires to the line posts on the windward side of the posts, which means toward the direction from which the wind blows. They need to be tight enough to

hold the wires in place, but with enough distance to allow the wire to be tightened.

Vine training systems

The best way to train your vines around the trellis depends on both the region you live in and the conditions in your home garden space. Different systems and strategies work for vines grown in colder climates than those grown in warmer areas. The best time to erect the trellis is either when the vines are planted, or when they have been established a year. From then on, training involves positioning the vines and removing unnecessary vegetative growth to prepare them for supporting vigorous fruit production in the coming years. There are many types of grapevine training systems that all have their own names, and many are derivatives of a few basic designs. All of the training systems that have been developed are meant to optimize the amount of direct sunshine that reaches the vines. Three of them will be discussed in this book because they are among the simplest but are still very effective.

The Single Curtain Cordon

The first is the Single Curtain Cordon system, which involves the least effort by the gardener. The cordons are trained to grow horizontally on either side of the trunk, along a single wire located high off the ground. The shoots and spurs that grow from those cordons are positioned to grow down vertically, creating a curtain. A curtain is the portion of the vine canopy that has been positioned according to a particular system of training on a selected trellis and usually hangs down. The canopy is the total complex of arms, leaves, and shoots of a grape vine. Hybrid grape varieties have produced well when trained into a single curtain, as described above. A hybrid is the result of a cross between two separate species of grapevines, usually done for the production of good wine grapes.

The Four Arm Kniffen

The Four Arm Kniffen design is used on a trellis that has two wires. The vine cordons are trained horizontally from the trunk in both directions, parallel to both wires. In this fashion, four arms are created. The arms are the main branches of the grape vine that extend from the trunk, and from them extend canes and spurs. A cane is a mature, woody shoot that still contains buds after a leaf falls off. A spur is a section of the cane that develops leaf and flower buds. This simple, two-wire system works best for vines of moderate vigor. Vines with lower vigor are trained on trellises with three wires. The productivity of vines with high vigor would be compromised with this system because the bottom arms would be shaded by the top growth.

The Fan System

The Fan System is a third type that is used to grow more fragile varieties in colder climate zones. The trellis for training these vines has three wires. One or more vine trunks are grown to at least a foot high. When the heads form, the shoots that develop from it grow upright, toward the top wire. The head is the top of a grapevine trunk, including the upper arms. As the shoots grow further and develop more, they are positioned as a fan across all three wires. This system is optimal for protecting the trunk during the colder winter months, and for renewal of the "fruiting canes" the following spring. A cane is a mature, woody shoot that still contains buds after a leaf falls off. It also refers to one-year-old fruiting vine wood.

PLANTING KIWIFRUIT

The kiwifruit is a vine fruit that migrated to the United States from around the world, with origins in Italy, China, and New Zealand before reaching the shores of North America. They are small, juicy, and irresistible as a snack. The dark green pulp inside the fuzzy brown skin is naturally sweet and the tiny black seeds add to the enjoyment of eating it because they are arranged in a pretty design at the center. Even the scientific name of the

kiwifruit acknowledges its flavor — *Actinidia deliciosa*. Although the kiwifruit most familiar to North Americans is the variety with the fuzzy skin, there are smooth-skinned varieties that also exist, as well as those with yellow flesh. Regardless of the texture of its skin, it is often enjoyed as an ingredient in fruit salad or fruit juice, and most often paired with the strawberry. Not only are they scrumptious, they are full of vitamin C and potassium.

Kiwifruit, like grapes and other vine fruit, grow best in soil that is acidic (pH 5.0 to 6.5), but they will not grow well in heavy soil that retains too much moisture. Instead, there needs to be a balance between sandy loam and dark organic material. A balanced amount of sunlight also favors kiwifruit, so if there is an area of your garden that is shaded for part of the day, your kiwifruit would flourish there. Many varieties of kiwifruit need at least 30 percent of their growth area shaded. Protecting them from wind is also important because the vine branches break easily when they are full of fruit. If you have a hedge or a small grove of trees near your garden, this feature can offer both the protection from the wind and amount of shade that the kiwi vines require for growth and production.

One final consideration before the planting process begins is that of cross-pollination. The kiwifruit plant grows both male and female flowers, which either produce pollen or receive it to make seeds with. No one flower does both, so they need the birds and the bees to transport the pollen between them. One helpful hint for the gardener who finds it necessary to hand-pollinate is that the male flowers are visibly larger than the female flowers. The larger flowers are the flowers from which to brush the pollen off the stamens, to place on the pistils of the smaller flowers.

Before planting kiwifruit vines directly into your garden, it is important to give them some time to grow in a pot. If the vines spend time growing in a 50/50 mix of potting soil and soil from your garden, they have time to adapt themselves gradually to their future growing environment. Keeping the kiwifruit cultivars in a pot above ground level in a warm room will hasten their readiness to produce a plentiful crop of fruit after they are planted outside.

When the trunk of the kiwifruit vine has a diameter of ½ inch and is between 3 and 6 feet high, it is ready for planting directly into your garden soil. The distance between them varies depending on the level of production vigor possessed by a particular variety. The range begins at 8 to 10 feet for more modest producers and extends to between 15 and 18 feet for varieties that offer a more vigorous yield. The average distance between rows is 15 feet.

The following is a list of tips to remember when planting kiwifruit:

1. While the plant is still dormant and after the final spring frost, dig a hole of the same depth as the plant grew at the nursery, and in the pot.

2. Pack soil around the roots, so it will keep them warm.

3. Refill the rest of the hole with the remaining soil, and continue packing.

4. Water the ground close to the plant thoroughly.

5. Prune back the vine so that the stem of the plant produces a single shoot that is 6 to 12 inches long.

6. Train the vine on a trellis to support the growth of flowers, leaves, and abundant fruit. Training the canopy onto a trellis with at least 3 wires is recommended because of the vigor of kiwifruit vines in general.

PLANTING RHUBARB

Rhubarb appears last in this planting series because it is neither a tree fruit nor a berry plant, but a hardy vegetable that grows in the form of red or green stalks, similar in shape to celery, and lasts up to 20 years. Originally used as a form of medicine in China and brought to Europe by Marco Polo 700 years ago, it is a member of the *Rheum* family, and the scientific name for garden rhubarb is *Rheum cultorum*. Despite the botanical classification as a vegetable, the flavor of rhubarb reminds many people of a very sour fruit. It is often referred to as the "pie plant" because that is the one way most people prepare it, using plenty of sugar. Sometimes cooks add strawberries or other small fruits with the rhubarb to add an extra fruity flavor and increase the natural sweetness of the pie.

Rhubarb will survive temperatures as low as -20 degrees Fahrenheit. A winter temperature that drops at least as low as 40 degrees Fahrenheit is necessary for the flower casings of the rhubarb plant to split and produce fresh growth. A temperature of at least 75 degrees Fahrenheit is vital to its production of healthy vegetation. It is generally cultivated and grown in the Northern states or in regions that experience a long, cool spring season. Rhubarb is as big as it is hardy and may grow to a size of two feet wide and six feet tall.

photo by Karen Szklany Gault

It is wise to give it plenty of room if you choose to grow it in your garden. If left to its own devices, rhubarb will grow back abundantly every year (perennially) for a couple of decades.

The types of soils that rhubarb enjoys most are acidic, with a pH between 5.5 and 6.5.

One of the most important elements to provide for the growth of rhubarb is plenty of sunshine, especially for plants with red stalks. Ample sunshine will ensure a more vibrant color and stronger flavor. Rhubarb also needs plenty of space to grow as it matures. A corner of the garden near other perennial edible-producing plants, such as asparagus, suits rhubarb well.

The best way to plant rhubarb is to place a ball of roots that has been split from an established plant into the ground and cover it with soil, including the crown with at least one bud. If only the seeds of its flowers are used, the plant may take longer to become established and produce quality fruit. It is important to transplant the entire rootstock.

Following are guidelines for planting rhubarb:

1. The hole dug for rhubarb roots needs to be about two feet in diameter and at least one foot deep. The distance between holes should be 1 to 2 feet apart, in rows that are 3 to 4 feet apart.

2. Place the root ball and crown in the hole and surround it with composted manure or peat moss.

3. Pack the soil firmly around the roots, but loosely around the buds.

4. Water the crowns of the plants after the holes have been re-filled with soil.

5. If your garden retains too much water in the soil, growing rhubarb in raised beds will protect it from the threat of too much moisture, which would make your plants more susceptible to diseases and pests.

photo by Karen Szklany Gault

6. After five years of growth, it is customary to thin the plant growth by splitting the roots and stems in the spring and transplanting them to a new bed.

photo by Karen Szklany Gault

Planting fruit trees and berry plants is hard work. When the sprinklers are watering your new garden, there is time to rest before the pruning begins. As your cultivars are slowly pushing forth buds, you may decide that this new fruit and berry passion deserves to spread out further, and manifest itself on your patio, porch, and sunroom. *Chapter 7 will give you ideas about how that can happen by using containers, and perhaps even keeping a greenhouse.*

photo by Ken Porter

CHAPTER 7

Container Gardening and Greenhouse Growing

ultivating fruit trees and berry plants in containers and greenhouses is a way of adding to the edible menagerie growing in your outside garden. Each of these mediums for growing fruits and berries has its own advantages. You can spread the charm of such lively company as strawberries or cranberries to other areas of your home, both inside and outside, by placing containers of them in strategic nooks and corners. They would make a final touch on your porch or patio, in a sunroom, or in your kitchen. Because containers are moveable, you are able to control how much daily sunlight your plants receive, and protect them from damage during storms or heat waves.

If containers are not enough to satisfy your new passion, a small greenhouse can be constructed to house your edibles-bearing plants all year round, and would be the place to grow some food that would not grow naturally in the prevailing climate where you live. You may want to try growing blueberries if you live in the Southwest or pineapples if you live in the New England states or Alaska. Depending upon the needs of the specific plants you would like to grow, the environment in the greenhouse can be controlled to stay cool or warm.

CONTAINER GARDENING

If you find that your gardening dreams have outgrown the space you have for planting fruits and berries, do not despair. There is a way to include that extra berry plant in your plans by growing it in a container. A container is moveable, so the gardener is able to determine the amount of direct sunlight a plant receives each day. Some gardeners have used shorter trellises to train grape or kiwi vines while growing them in containers. Dwarf fruit trees, such as those that grow lemons, limes, oranges, or kumquats, are also an option for those of you with very sunny corners of your yard or patio, or even your living room. If you are a gardener who would like to grow your own fruit for purposes of both economy and sustainability, you will find that using containers for some of that growing can turn your gardening dreams into reality. The results of this endeavor will be worth the containers that support your fruit plants, because it will save you the cost of buying fruits and berries at the grocery store. This is also what makes growing your own food sustainable, because no fuel is used to walk to your own garden. Composting kitchen scraps and other organic materials to create and feed the soil of your plants instead of throwing it all away in plastic bags is another way that growing your own fruits and berries organically is environmentally sustainable.

Not only will you have an abundance of your own fruit to eat, but that fruit also will be of the highest quality because it is home grown. The taste of commercially produced fruit can be compromised by being picked before they are truly ripe. Growing your own fruits and berries instead, and eating them fresh from the source, is the sweetest deal in town.

Some of you who may find container growing to be your only gardening option live in regions with harsh climates, such as deserts or plains, where long periods of drought and frequent, strong winds pose a threat to the survival of trees and bushes planted in the ground. Even those who live in regions friendlier to in-ground gardening may experience extreme weather conditions, such as the occasional thunderstorm or hurricane, from which they will need to protect their plants. Gardeners can protect their plants by bringing those that grow in containers to a more sheltered corner of their property or even inside. Those who experience very cold winters may find it possible to grow fruit all year round by transporting their plants to a warmer area of their homes during those colder months.

The transportability of containers makes them perfect for use on patios, porches, balconies, staircase landings, and the rooftops of apartment buildings. Those who live in a city, no matter what region it is located in, will appreciate the ability to create a movable feast with fruit grown in containers. The containers can be moved and rearranged in a wide variety of patterns according to color, texture, shape, design, or the type of fruit plants growing in them. Wherever they are kept, both the containers and plants will add an extra splash of year-round ornamentation to the corner of your home or garden where they rest. No matter what type of containers you use and no matter where you decide to place them, the plants you grow in them will need to be watered. In addition to the choice of vessels available for planting in, there are watering cans designed especially for use with hanging plants, in addition to those designed for pots, tubs, or beds that lie closer to the ground. Yet, the means of watering your plants may be the easy part. The challenge might be in determining the correct type of container in which to plant a particular type of fruit so that it will flourish and yield fruit.

Types of containers and what they are used for

Different types of containers are used for specific varieties of fruit plants. They will need to support the plants you decide to grow for their entire lives if you do not intend to transplant them into the soil of an outside garden. This means that the roots must be given the nutrients and space to support the growth and maturity of the plants that are meant to develop, flower, and bear fruit above the soil that feeds them. Any container used for a tree will need to be bigger than one used for a bush, and those that house

vines will need to be both longer and wider than those in which a single berry plant, such as a variety of strawberry, will grow. You may need to decide which comes first in your budget, the container or the plant, because purchasing the

containers that are big enough to support root growth is vitally important to your fruit-gardening success. One strategy for determining the size of a needed container would be to measure the root system of the plant that it is intended for and purchase a pot with twice that circumference. The nursery that you purchase your fruit cultivars from may be able to give you special instructions regarding the care of plants grown in containers, such as which varieties of each fruit are best grown that way. They may even sell the containers and be able to give you an idea of the minimum size that will be required by each plant.

Pots

Pots are generally used for growing individual dwarf trees or bushes. Straw-berries also grow well in pots of various sizes. Trees, brambles, or bushes grown in pots will need extra attention because their root systems are small-er than those planted in the ground. They will need to be watered more often because less water is absorbed into the plant through the roots. The

variety of blueberry bush most often grown in containers is a dwarf version called "tophat." A pot with a 12 to 15 inch diameter is the average size to use for growing them. Alpine strawberry varieties are also good candidates for growing in pots because they run small and do not produce runners, so they do not use up the nutrients in the soil as quickly. The average size pot to use is 6 inches in diameter.

Hanging baskets

Baskets designed for hanging plants often add extra ornamentation to the garden, patio, porch, or apartment rooftop. They are good for protecting plants and fruit from furry friends, because they take more work to ap-proach and pillage. Now that there are watering cans designed especially for use with hanging plants, the process of caring for them is as easy as for plants in containers that stay on the ground, even for gardeners who are vertically challenged. Strawberry plants, which are related to roses, look beautiful and produce well in hanging baskets.

Tubs

Tubs are used for rows of several plants of a similar type that have compatible needs for particular amounts of sunshine and moisture. They are a good place for planting several varieties of the same species of fruit bush for the purpose of cross-pollination. Long tubs, such as window boxes, may be used creatively to support the growth of grape and kiwi vines. Shorter trellises, often made of wood or plastic, may be placed firmly in the soil and the vine cordons trained around them. You may even want to make your own trellis with a fancy design.

Raised beds

Raised beds are basically giant frames of various shapes. They are usually placed on land that is not ready to support in-ground planting and are

simple to assemble. The basic shapes for raised beds are the square and rectangle. But other shapes may appeal to you, as well, such as octagon, hexagon, trapezoid, rhombus, and triangle. The tools needed for their construction are wood, hammer, and nails, or a kit from your local home improvement store.

Earth boxes

The Earth Box™ is a kit with a specific name and designer. It is a container gardening starter kit that includes a tub, a water-fill tube, rolling casters for easy movement, soil amendment mix, and fertilizer. The gardener needs to supply only the soil and the desired seedlings or cultivar. Its earthy green color is complementary to a variety of design schemes, so it is likely to blend in well with some of the other containers you already have. Detailed information about the design of the box, its assembly, and the supplies that accompany it are described at **www.earthbox.com/consumer/instructions.html**. The average price per Earth Box™ is $40.

Container planting

The process for planting in containers is simple, and similar to in-ground planting.

1. Prepare the potting soil mix you want to use for the specific fruit you will be planting.

2. Tap the side of the temporary pot that the plant was purchased in to remove the root ball and the soil surrounding it.

3. Make sure the container is located in a place it can stay for a minimum of 30 days, while the plant become established there.

4. Place a thin layer of soil at the bottom of the pot, then place the root system of the plant on that soil, making sure there are 2 inches of space on all sides between the roots and the inside wall of the container.

5. Spread the roots out on the bottom of the pot and pack a layer of soil around them.

6. Fill the pot with the soil, leaving about 2 inches from the top free so that none of the soil will be lost when the pot is filled with water.

7. Water the soil thoroughly.

Sources for obtaining containers

There are many creative options for obtaining containers for growing fruits and berries. In addition to hardware stores, gardening centers, and other home-improvement destinations, there are craft fares and second-hand swap meet events that offer unique, inexpensive items for sale. If you are working on a shoestring budget, you may want to consider creating containers with recycled materials, such as plastic gallon jugs, jars, and other refuse left unused by others. Freecycle is also a source of free supplies, at **www.freecycle.org**.

Spaces to put the containers

If you are wondering where to put your gardening containers once you have filled them with fruit and berry plants, there are places to congregate containers of similar sizes, shapes, or designs around a larger structure. Here are three examples:

Fountains

Setting containers on a water fountain will give the lucky plants in them the chance to receive more moisture than they normally would. The mist from the fountain will keep them watered gently while they adorn your garden feature. Layered fountains give you more surface area to play with.

Statues

A favorite statue or sculpture may enjoy having several potted plants close by.

Benches

Bench seats for reading, drawing, or reflecting are the best places to put a few plants grown in containers. The plants and fruit are beautiful to see and the fruit is easy to nibble while you sit, either alone or with a friend. A bench that swings may provide additional pleasure to your garden.

CASE STUDY:
OUTRAGEOUS GARDENING
WITH RECYCLED MATERIALS

Yvonne Scott is a container gardener who lives in the north valley of Albuquerque, New Mexico. Her home is located in the high desert, at 4,500 feet above sea level, which can become very windy. The summers there are very hot.

Scott has long been a fan of container gardening because of its flexibility. "Because of all the variety of soils, especially in the city," she said. "I was drawn to any type of gardening that did not require digging in the ground, and I could still create the best growing medium possible." She has grown strawberries and blueberries successfully in containers.

When asked what types of containers she uses for growing fruits and berries, Scott responded that she "recycles a variety of materials that are light enough to move plants around to different patches of sunlight throughout the day, or heavy and strong enough to withstand high winds."

Raised beds are created with car tires, which she calls "Lasagna Beds" because of the way she layers the organic mulch and compost materials into the bed to form the appropriate soil for each of her plants. She explained further that, "one of the very best reasons to create raised beds, or 'lasagna beds,' is the ability to bypass all the contortions over whether [the soil] is sandy, clay, loam, alkaline, or acid. It does not make any difference. The complexity of the organic matter in the bed over time mitigates all those concerns."

Other recycled materials she uses to make her raised beds are bricks and stones. The stones she uses to make smaller beds, which she calls "keyhole gardens." Plastic wading pools for children, plastic gallon jugs, and burlap bags have also been used. The Growmaker™ bag is highly recommended, particularly for starting berries, nut, or fruit trees. "My preference from a sustainability perspective is burlap bags. They decompose readily so that you can plant the entire bag [in a bed] and not worry about root girdling." Root girdling is a condition that container-grown trees are susceptible to, where roots grow over the main stem of the tree and restrict further growth so that the tree dies.

Scott is the creator of a concept she calls "Outrageous Gardening," where people learn to grow food in recycled containers close to their homes. She travels to different countries that experience weather patterns that are not conducive to keeping gardens planted directly into the ground, and gives workshops to aspiring gardeners. These are often people in poor, underdeveloped countries with a high poverty rate. Her mission is to teach the people she works with to rely on their own personal resources for meeting their needs. Scott encourages them to scout for materials that are inexpensive and easy to find, and therefore dispensable after harvesting season. "Containers make it easier to dive into gardening and experiment with new plants," Scott said. "To be able to use found materials with little labor investment makes it more enticing to try things." If one plant does not work out, the container is often used for something else. "And the soil of one plant may become the compost for another the following season," Scott added.

To learn more about Scott's ongoing work, visit her inspiring blog, at **www.outrageousgardens.com**. Her gardening students have found this simple means of growing their own fruits, nuts, and berries as food for themselves very liberating. In addition to those efforts, they grow trees from seedlings in hanging burlap bags and sell them as a source of income.

GREENHOUSE GROWING

Imagine being able to walk through aisles of green, leafy plants that grow edible fruit while the rest of the world is blanketed under inches of winter snow outside. Nestled inside a warm house that uses solar energy, and other sustainable heat sources to grow fruits and berries, you can sit down on a bench or at a table to sip tea and eat a fresh fruit parfait or salad, draw, write, or read in your private garden. This would be your own piece of paradise, and it is possible to experience such repose in a greenhouse.

The ability to experience beauty in the middle of winter weather might be one reason you might consider growing fruits and berries in a greenhouse. The plants that grow edible crops, such as fruits, nuts, and berries, are beautiful themselves, and the fruit they produce only adds to their beauty. Yet, the most important reason that you may have to decide to construct a greenhouse is the freedom it offers for growing fruits and berries year-round. Strawberries, raspberries, blackberries, and blueberries may keep producing new buds and fruit to add to salads and pies all twelve months of the year. In addition to this, it gives you the opportunity to grow

photo by Karen Szklany Gault

fruits and berries that normally flourish in climates that are very different than your own. If you live in New England, that might mean mandarin oranges for ambrosia salads, Mexican limes for margaritas and guacamole dips, and even the avocados themselves, or pineapples for sweet grilled kebabs. Your world has just blossomed before you because you are considering the possibility of constructing a greenhouse.

Greenhouse design and construction

You may have room for a freestanding greenhouse on your property, or there may be another type of greenhouse design of a different shape and size that meets your needs while providing as much pleasure. Such a construction might be a smaller extension of your house, or an enclosed window box that you can see from your bedroom or study. The shape of your house or the amount of space you have around your home may determine which design will work best for you. There are a variety of greenhouses and tunnels in a variety of sizes that you can build, either from raw materials or from an assembly of materials provided for you. This section describes the types of greenhouses that you may build for growing fruits and berries year-round.

"Dutch" greenhouse

A Dutch greenhouse is the traditional freestanding greenhouse design. Glass is encased in a metal frame, which reaches down from an apex with an obtuse angle, with the sides angled out a bit further from the middle. The shape is like a triangle sitting on top of a trapezoid. The angles of the sides are designed to add structural support to the entire building. The glass traps and stores the light and heat energy of the sun in order to keep the temperature inside high enough to support trees and other plants accustomed to growing in regions with warmer average temperatures than those of the atmosphere outside the greenhouse.

Wide-span A-frame

Bearing a more modern appearance, this freestanding greenhouse design has a triangular, "A-frame" shape. All the panes around the frame are glass, but solar reflection shutters can be added, and moved with a pulley system. The shutters will need to be braced firmly in order to withstand strong winds.

Window greenhouse

Taking the shape of a small greenhouse constructed off a corner room that bears a window or two, the window greenhouse is built adjacent to the side of a house. It may lead to a deck that is also constructed directly outside the greenhouse windows, with a door that leads from the greenhouse to the deck, and stairs leading from the deck to the ground. A homeowner with this design may enjoy the greenhouse from both the inside and the outside, and even walk through the "greenhouse room" to leave the house.

Window-box greenhouse

The idea of a window box is taken a step further with this design. It is a greenhouse that is made of windows, and attached to the outside of a house below a window. The small greenhouse is filled with soil laden with leafy plants. The only types of fruit that may flourish successfully in a window box greenhouse are berries that do not require cross-pollination to produce fruit, such as strawberries, blackberries, and raspberries. This arrangement gives the plants plenty of sun for minimal effort.

Lean-to greenhouse

Attached to the side of a house at ground level, a greenhouse with a lean-to design can double as a sunroom. Roll-up shades are often attached to the outside of the frame, which are used to control the amount of light and heat allowed into the building. Because it is usually constructed to function as an additional room to a building, it may serve as a room for entertaining guests, or spending a quiet afternoon reading. In addition to providing an oasis from the everyday work world, it could also serve as a sunny studio for an artist, architect, or writer.

The greenhouse designs described previously use glass as the medium to admit the sun's light and heat. However, there are other designs that may cost even less than those and use plastic as the medium to permit passage to the sun's rays and store their energy, rather than glass. Some of the designs may be similar to those discussed here and some may have new designs, but there is bound to be one that appeals to you.

Mobile greenhouse tunnel

A moveable greenhouse on wheels may serve as an asset to gardeners who would like to save money by not having to heat their greenhouses with a source of warmth in addition to the sun. The tunnel is moved on wheels over a track, so it can absorb the strongest rays of the sun by managing its position on your property. The shape of the tunnel frame is a long semicircle formed by a series of arched cables. A material made of plastic is spread across the frame to absorb the light and heat energy of the sun. Gardeners who use this greenhouse model usually stagger their plant cultivation so that certain seedlings are germinated sooner to give a head start to their season of production, such as lettuce and tomatoes. Fruit crops are kept warm in order to also produce beyond their usual length of season, such as strawberries.

Heating equipment

Heating equipment is generally used to increase the temperature of a greenhouse. The direct result of this effort is an increase in the range of fruits and berries you will be able to grow in it. The three types of heaters used most are paraffin, gas, and electric. A paraffin heater uses a wick and produces a blue flame. It is available in a portable can, but it is infamous for producing a fume. There are extra costs associated with gas heaters because they need to be installed and the level of gas must be maintained for proper functioning of the heater. Electric heaters may be the "greenest" of them all because they are the most reliable and no energy is wasted in their use. Boilers with hot water pipe systems have also been used. Those are the most expensive and least sustainable because they rely on fuel to run. Hot water heaters alone are useful when growing citrus trees, because the tree must stay warm and the water heater provides the warmth needed for their survival and productivity, both in the air temperature maintained by the heater and the moisture they receive through the condensation it produces.

Fruits and berries that are grown in a greenhouse

The temperature maintained in the greenhouse will determine the types of fruits and berries you will be able to grow and enjoy year-round. The heating equipment above can be used to manage the temperature that you would like to maintain in your greenhouse. There are four basic types of greenhouse temperature ranges that will encourage fruit plants to grow that are accustomed to growing under those conditions. In addition to these distinctions, greenhouse growers have split big greenhouses into two or more growing ranges.

Cool greenhouse

The minimum temperature kept is between 40 and 45 degrees Fahrenheit. This temperature range is good for preserving fruit plants during their period of dormancy.

Intermediate house

The minimum temperature for this type of greenhouse is 50 degrees Fahrenheit. More fruit plants will grow and produce in this temperature than those in the cooler greenhouse. A few examples are citrus trees and mangos.

Warm greenhouse

The minimum temperature for a warm greenhouse is 60 degrees Fahrenheit. Tropical fruits such as the kiwi will grow and produce successfully in this temperature.

Stove house

The minimum temperature for the "stove" house is 70 degrees Fahrenheit, so this is the most expensive type of greenhouse to maintain due to the cost of the energy to keep it heated. It is not used as often anymore, because the plants that grow in a "stove" house will also grow in a warm greenhouse.

CASE STUDY:
RAISING TOMATOES FROM
SEEDLINGS IN GREENHOUSES

Steen Bentzen has been growing tomato seedlings in greenhouses for the past 20 years. He sells the seedlings at farmers' markets near Boston with his partner Carla Montague. They live and work at their home in Berlin, Massachusetts, named "Great Oak Farm." Native to Denmark, Bentzen has also grown strawberries, gooseberries, and currants.

Bentzen built both greenhouses that stand on his property. The small one is 10 feet by 45 feet, and the bigger one is 27 feet by 50 feet. "The top is round so that the snow falls off, or else it would crush the greenhouse," Bentzen added.

He described his method for constructing the greenhouses:

1. Create the frame by attaching the metal poles to the wooden base, and make the shape of the house with them.

2. Place a double layer of plastic over the frame as the insulation.

3. Install a thermostat to regulate the internal temperature of the house, and a fan to blow the hot air out.

4. The vents in the wall at one end of the house open and a fan starts when the temperature becomes too warm.

5. A propane heater is used on winter nights to keep the temperature at 40 degrees Fahrenheit, and is turned off each morning.

Bentzen is an electrical engineer, so he also built the temperature control system that regulates the environment in the larger greenhouse. "Tomato seedlings are kept at a temperature between 75 and 80 degrees Fahrenheit," he said. The seedlings are germinated and grown from seeds of different varieties.

The progression of sowing the tomato seeds works from the bottom up. The seed trays are placed on tables in the greenhouse and the planting soil made of peat and loam is placed in piles in the trays. A block cutter is used to make 20 square blocks of soil with a hole in the middle of each block. One seed tray holds 80 blocks of soil. Montague uses a wet toothpick to pick up each seed and place it in the hole of one of the soil blocks.

When the tomato seedlings are 2 inches high, they are placed in cold frames outside the greenhouse, so that they will adapt further to the climate of the region. The cold frames are made of a bed that holds the trays, with glass on top, and poles with netting and plastic placed over them to cover the seed trays. The covering aids the frame in capturing the sun and protects the seedlings from frost. If Bentzen wants to hasten the germination process, he places them on an incubator first, and warms them with a heating pad from below. "Seedlings can also be placed on a window sill to germinate," he added.

Before 10 o'clock in the morning or after 3 in the afternoon every 3 or 4 days, Bentzen sprays the foliage of the tomato plants with a water and fish fertilizer mix. Those are the times of day when the pores on the plant leaves are open and most receptive to this type of irrigation. When the seedlings are 6 inches high and the final New England frost is behind them, they are planted in the ground on Bentzen's farm. Because he is a commercial seller, he has a planting machine, a type of tractor with two "ribbons" spaced 21 inches apart, which make two rows of holes for placing the soil blocks with the seedlings in them. "Those with a small backyard garden can dig the holes with a small spade," he said.

As a final parting thought, Bentzen also noted that "fruit cultivars can also be kept in the greenhouse before you are ready to plant them." It is a good place to keep them while the ground is still too frosty to dig.

photo by Karen Szklany Gault

Because tomatoes are considered a fruit by many botanists, they are referred to as such for this book. They are only one of the many fruits that may be raised from seeds, using a greenhouse to keep and care for them. All of the fruits that have been discussed in this guide, and many more, may be grown in either containers or a greenhouse, but the majority of fruit and berry plants will yield their best crops with longer seasons in a greenhouse. Another advantage of both container gardening and greenhouse growing is that you will not have any weeding to do. Both are easier on your back than in-ground growing and leave you more time for enjoying their beauty. No matter how you grow your own fruits and berries, both you and the earth will win, because the more food you grow, the fewer trips to the grocery store you will need to take, and the more you will be able to share with friends. Yet, for all forms of gardening, there is still some ongoing care that needs to be given to your plants, and the next chapter will discuss the methods for practicing that care.

CHAPTER 8

Ongoing Care

Once your trees are planted and on their way to blossoming and bearing fruit, it is important to provide them with ongoing care. They need to be kept moist, protected from unexpected frost, and relieved of the burden of dead and unproductive branches. The extent to which you keep them comfortable and healthy throughout their lives will determine how well they will reward you with many seasons of abundant fruit crops.

GENERAL CARE

The most general care that trees and plants need throughout their growing season includes weeding, pruning, fertilizing, and watering. Within that realm of general care, different types of fruit and berry plants require a customized schedule. The weeding will be ongoing, but watering can vary, depending on how moist the plants require their soil to be. Plants that favor an acidic soil will require more watering than those that are more comfortable in neutral soil, and even less for alkaline. Fruits that grow on vines will need to be trained around trellises. Fruits and berries kept in containers might need to be moved because the angle of direct sunlight that shines upon your yard changes over the course of the season. Use the following information to learn about caring for the types of fruit you will be raising.

Sunlight

Making sure that all fruit trees and berry plants receive ample sunlight will ensure a plentiful harvest. In addition to pollination, sunlight is vital to fruit production. Photosynthesis is a key process that supports all fruit plants in that endeavor. Ongoing care must facilitate each tree, vine, bramble, and bush to receive enough sunlight and pruning is a very important activity for making sure that happens.

Watering

The first three or four weeks after planting are the most important for providing adequate moisture to your fruit trees and berry plants. The water is a conduit for the nutrients present in the soil to reach the plants, and this helps them become established in your garden through root and stem growth. Using a hose to provide a steady trickle into the soil close to the trunk is the most effective method for doing this. If your garden hose does not reach far enough, a sprinkler set so that the water gives that same area a frequent shower may be the next best strategy for getting that moisture to them.

Fertilizing

photo by Sarah Florreich

The type of fertilizer you use for each type of fruit tree or berry plant will differ, depending on the nutrients that plant needs most. Some need more phosphorus, others more potassium or nitrogen. However, raking worm castings, organic manure, and fully decomposed materials from your compost pile into the soil will provide all the nutrients that all plants need. Fruit trees and bushes need to be watered before and after fertilizer is applied. Before application of the organic materials, the water softens the ground so that the new material seeps more deeply into the soil when it is applied. Afterward, the water becomes a natural vehicle for the nutrients to reach the roots.

Weeding

Weeding is crucial for allowing all the nutrients in the soil to get to your fruit trees. Weeds pose serious competition for those nutrients. This is why it is important to surround the tree with mulch materials, like wood chips, that suppress the growth of grass and weeds that take away from the food the tree is supposed to be using. Preventative measures save the most time. If the planting area for all fruit and berry cultivars is cleared of weeds from the level of their roots before the those plants are placed in the ground, they are not likely to reappear and cause you trouble in the weeks ahead. Removing the weeds also reduces the risk of your fruit trees and berry plants developing microscopic pests and diseases and will prolong their lives and productivity.

Citrus trees

Weeding is especially important for maintaining healthy citrus tree growth. There needs to be a large area of bare soil surrounding the tree, which needs to maintain adequate moisture for the tree to grow. Organic mulch materials such as hay and wood chips would not benefit the citrus tree. They aid the retention of water instead of helping it drain, which is what citrus trees need. Therefore, it is best to leave this area clear of those materials. Frequent, deep weeding with a hand fork is better for the growth of healthy, productive citrus trees.

Berry plants

One strategy for suppressing the growth of weeds around berry bushes is to lay down straw around the plants as the fruit is forming. This is especially true for strawberry bushes. Barley straw is the first choice to use with them among veteran fruit growers, and wheat straw is the second choice. The straw also keeps the ground moist and warm for the plants.

Pruning

Pruning is the removal of dead or unproductive branches from a tree. The canopy of a fruit tree will need to be maintained with pruning so that the most productive branches receive enough sunlight to develop flower buds that blossom and produce fruit. Grape and kiwi vines will need to be pruned so that the higher cordons on a trellis system do not overshadow others, and thus limit their productivity. Bramble canes will need to be managed closely through pruning so that they do not overstep their boundaries in your garden and take nutrients away from your other fruit trees and berry plants.

photo by Edward S. Gault

There are different systems of pruning unique to the type of plant you are working with. This means that you would approach pruning a fruit tree differently than you would a bush or a vine, including the use of different tools. Wearing your garden gloves will help prevent injury to your hands.

Fruit trees

There are two times in the growth cycle of a fruit tree that it is customary to prune and train it. Pruning refers to the cuts made in order to trim back branches and shoots. The pattern of your pruning will "train" your tree to grow in a particular pattern during the summer. The first is while it is dormant, during the cooler months of the year. The other time is during the summer, when it is actively growing and producing leaves, flowers, and fruit. If too much of the tree is pruned during its dormancy, the tree may respond by growing abundant vegetation (leaves) and little or no fruit. It may also send shoots straight up that will shade the rest of the tree, preventing the lower branches from receiving the sunshine that they need.

If a tree is pruned too early in its summer growth cycle, its potential for further growth may be reduced. When summer pruning is done, the cuts should be small, thinning cuts from branches that have already grown leaves. Such pruning activity is best done before August, because any cutting done after the end of July could render the tree vulnerable to damage from an early frost.

The growth cycle and age of the tree are also very important to the timing of dormant pruning. Older trees will be able to withstand early pruning better than younger trees, so they are the ones to prune first. Within that scheme, trees that blossom later, such as apple and pecan, should be pruned first. Those that bloom sooner, such as cherry, peach, and plum, should be pruned last. This is because the later-blooming trees are less vulnerable to harm from the cold than those that bloom first. They stay dormant longer because their growth and production cycle is later.

The pruning cuts made to peripheral growth shoots are done at a downward angle, leaving no stub protruding from the lateral branch that the shoots are cut from. The downward angle prevents water from settling into the cut site and causing it to rot. Cutting close to the lateral branch from which the shoot is taken so that no stub is left behind will ensure that the site will heal faster, because it will be closer to the central growth energy of the tree. The sooner the pruning cut heals, the less likely the tree will succumb to attack by either pests or disease.

Use the following steps for pruning a fruit tree:

1. Leave only one central trunk, called the "leader."

2. Remove branches that are at less than a 60-degree angle to the trunk.

3. Remove branches that are directly across from each other across the leader.

4. Space out lateral branches to prevent crowding during growth and production.

Melons

Melons are not generally pruned. Instead, they are continually trained as they are grown from seeds, often on a trellis because they are vines. The gardener usually pinches the buds to encourage more leaf and flower growth. This facilitates pollination so that fruit may form.

Berries

No pruning is necessary for any of the plants that bear berries during their summer growth season. Most of them are trained on vines, but they are all treated alike in the fall after their fruit has been harvested. Between November and March, prune the central canes of raspberries and blackberries down to about 12 inches from the ground, with no peripheral branches kept, to encourage fresh growth in the spring. They will then be ready to train on their trellises all over again. The same is done with the branches of blueberries, currants, and other bush berries, and to the cordons of grape and kiwifruit vines.

```
CASE STUDY:
CARING FOR FRUIT TREES
AND BERRY BUSHES
AS A LABOR OF LOVE
```

Ralph "Chick" Papile has provided care to his pear trees and raspberry canes in his New England home garden for 45 years. Strawberries and peaches also grew in his garden for some of those years. He has found pleasure in the entire process of nurturing plants and watching them flourish in response to his care.

Papile plants his fruits and berries on the south side of his garden so that they receive at least 3 hours of sunlight each day. He keeps his raspberry bushes at least three feet apart and staggered between two rows so that there is room to move around them when it is time to harvest the fruit.

The fertilizer Papile prefers to use is one that he adds when planting, which slowly releases nutrients to enrich the soil. "Anything with equal parts nitrogen, potassium, and phosphorus is going to enrich the soil," he said.

"I also mulch," Papile added. "I make my own with whatever I have that is handy and pesticide free, like dried grass clippings, seaweed, or dried leaves." He also uses the grass clippings to discourage weeds from growing, by placing them as a covering on the ground around the plants, but not directly against the trunk so that there is room for watering.

To save water, Papile collects rain in a barrel to use when his fruit plants need it. He also takes measures to help the soil retain the water it receives. "When they were planted, I put peat moss and other absorbing mulch in the bottom so they hold water. I water about once a week, then cover with grass clippings to hold the water."

Papile uses sharp pruning shears to prune tree branches. "For berries, you can use smaller ones," he added. When asked about his method, he advised, "Always prune the branches that are growing down on the bushes and trees. Try to leave enough ventilation and space so light can come down through the tree or bush."

With regard to timing, Papile said, "around here I like to prune fruit trees during the January thaw. We usually have one [in New England]. I like to do it then because the trees are still asleep. If you do it too far into the spring, the sap will be running and the trees will bleed."

Papile's pear trees are 70 years old and just stopped producing for him. "They stopped producing a couple of years ago. They used to give about three to five bushels a year," he said. "Each [raspberry] plant yields at least 1 quart of berries a season." He lets them re-root every two years. Each winter he removes old growth from them and uses that to enrich the soil.

LOW-TEMPERATURE CLIMATE CARE

As the global climate continues to change, gardeners will continue to face the dilemma of protecting their food-bearing plants from extreme weather conditions and sudden fluctuations in temperature. These are the events that kill trees. Midwinter thaws may warm trees out of dormancy, and the next ice storm or blizzard will freeze the tree past the point of recovery. This damage is usually invisible to the gardener until the spring, when no more life grows from the tree. Occasionally there may be a sign of damage, such as a cracked trunk.

Although global climate change can be a culprit in the case of a gardener losing a fruit tree, the protection from such loss begins at the time of garden planning. One of the pieces in the puzzle of being an effective gardener of fruit trees and berry plants is choosing the right material to work with. That is one reason why finding as small and as local a nursery as possible that sells such plants is a giant step in the right direction. This type of plant cultivator is most likely to be the one who works with trees that are acclimated to the area where the nursery is located, such as New England or the Midwest. The varieties of trees that are sold at that nursery may be that which will grow best in your own garden.

Another step in the planning process that may also lead you to your intended destination is to find your state horticultural society or university department of horticulture to find out which varieties are best suited to specific regions of the country. They might also be able to point you in the direction of those who sell these plants, if they do not themselves. The plants that you will choose and purchase will have growth and dormancy cycles that match the climate patterns of your home region. This alone is usually enough prevention to last a lifetime. Purchasing the appropriate varieties of the fruits you are passionate about growing can only make you and your plants happy and productive in the years to come. Bon voyage.

Dormancy

In the months soon after the fruit is harvested from the trees, bushes, brambles, or vines of your garden, fruit plants experience a period of dormancy. Their lifeblood slows down, eventually stops, and they enter a deep sleep. Your trees hibernate for the colder months of the year so that they may survive the winter and produce fresh buds, leaves, flowers, and fruit the following season. If this did not happen, they would continually produce buds that are tender, which would most likely die without ever bearing fruit. As a result, the tree could also soon die. Instead, the plants conserve their energy for the warmer months when the resources they need to produce fruit are available, such as abundant sunshine, water, mulch, fertilizer, and bees.

The items on your to-do list for preparing your trees for dormancy will differ tremendously with your list for preparing for the spring. Fertilizer is not applied in the fall because it delays dormancy and puts the trees at risk for frost damage.

Your steps to take for preparing for the winter should look similar to this:

1. Prune all your fruit plants back to their central leaders, trunks, or canes.

2. Place a light winter seed cover down on the soil and work it in with a garden rake.

3. Cover the winter seed with a layer of hay or grass clippings to keep the heat in the soil.

4. Bring all container-grown trees and bushes inside for the winter and place them in sunny spots around your home.

Protection from frost

Although trees enter their deep sleep, called "dormancy," they may still need some extra protection in the form of a covering that will keep them warm. Young trees will need to be protected by different methods than older trees that have matured and become more acclimated to your garden, and thus hardier.

Young fruit trees

Young trees are still tender. Their trunks have not hardened yet, so they need extra protection from frost damage during the winter months. The method used by most seasoned fruit tree gardeners to keep them warm when the temperature dips on winter nights is to provide a makeshift covering that is easily assembled and disassembled. The entire apparatus is meant to trap the warmth provided by the soil and some jugs of warm water as a balance against below-freezing temperatures. Young berry bushes may be protected in the same way.

These are the steps to take:

1. Cover the entire canopy of the tree with a tarp that reaches down to the ground.

2. If a tarp is not handy, tape together plastic bags to cover that area.

3. Use a ladder to place the cover over the canopy of the tree.

4. Weigh down the tarp or plastic covering with rocks, bricks, or anything else that is heavy enough to withstand a strong winter wind.

5. Place gallon jugs three-quarters full of warm water around the tree, inside the small tent you have created.

6. Remove the jugs and covering during the day if the temperature climbs above freezing so that the tree does not suffer damage from

extreme heat, and replace them at night when the temperature is predicted to dip back down again.

Mature fruit trees

Coating the trunk of the tree and heavy branches with water is usually done before the temperature dips below freezing. The light covering of water turns to ice quickly and forms a protective layering, like glass, that insulates the tree from the colder temperatures brought by nightfall. It will usually melt as the temperature becomes warmer, and will need to be reapplied when it is predicted to dip back down below freezing again.

Some types of fruit-plant care can be as strenuous as they are pleasurable, such as shoveling compost and pruning. If all tasks are completed with respect for the life cycles of the plants, they will reward you handsomely. In return for your gentle stewardship, they will give you many seasons of pleasure in the form of beauty, shade, and a bounty of delicious food.

CHAPTER 9

· · · · · · · · · ·

Pests
and Diseases

Pests and diseases cause great harm to both your fruit plants and their potential for yielding healthy crops. Pests often suck the lifeblood (sap) out of your plants and leave diseases that cause extensive loss in exchange. One of the first steps you can take to avoid such trouble and heartache is to personally visit the nursery, garden center, or farm that sells fruit trees and other fruit cultivars. While you are there, look carefully at the plants they sell. The plants you are looking for are about 1 year old and are about 1 inch in diameter. Their leaves and their root balls will each bear markers that indicate their state of health. If they look full and well cared for, (meaning their buds and leaves look fresh and their roots moist) then they are ready to take home. If they have any symptoms that cause concern, such as leaves that are discolored or a trunk marked with blemishes, they are best left alone.

PURCHASING HEALTHY CULTIVARS

Examine the plants you see at nurseries with care, because their overall health will indicate how well the staff attends to their needs and prepares them for life in a new home. When you find a variety of fruit or berry that seems like a good fit for you, look closely at its shape, its buds, and leaves, and take it out of the pot it is in to examine the roots and the ball of soil that surrounds it. Trust your instinct about what you see. If the plant seems happy and healthy, there is a good chance that it is. On the other hand, if there are discolorations and dryness, it is not in very good shape. The chart below provides the basic indicators that a cultivar is unhealthy, and thus unfit for transplanting to your outside garden, a container, or a greenhouse.

Shopping for Healthy Fruit Plants

Symptom	Problem
Yellowing leaves	Possibly pest-infested or diseased; or has nutrient deficiency
Wilted leaves	Temporarily stressed by too little water; neglected
Chewed leaves; sticky residues; webs, spots; distorted leaf or crown; mushy foliage;	Insect pest; disease
Scars or nicks in branches of woody plants	Branches or stems damaged; could point to or lead to disease.
Spindly growth	Poor light conditions; plant has outgrown pot it is in; has not been pruned or pinched properly
Poor color	Distress
Few roots and lots of soil	Weak; may not survive transplant
Roots growing out of bottom of pot	Distress from neglect
Weeds	Nutrient deficiency
Dry soil and root ball	Lifeless; may not be saved by transplanting

*Source: *How to Buy Healthy Plants: Problems to Avoid When Buying Garden Plants,* by Colleen Vanderlinden, at **http://organicgardening.about.com/od/startinganorganicgarden/a/healthyplants.htm**

PESTS

. . . .

Pests that wreak havoc on your garden are insects that are barely detectable by humans with the naked eye. However small they are, those little critters can do a world of damage to your plants, and cause monumental loss of fruit crops. They are very different from the critters that benefit your soil by breaking down organic materials that feed your plants good nutrients. Yet, it is difficult to distinguish between the good and bad among creatures you cannot see.

Although some small insects are bad news to have in your garden, there is one insect that is very visible, and it is good to see one crawling around the stems and leaves of your fruit plants because it is the natural enemy of the pests that would damage them. That beneficent bug is the "ladybug." The ladybug is classified as a member of the beetle *(Coccinellidae)* family. Some ladybugs feed on plant leaves, but most feed on the bugs and diseases that would otherwise attack your fruit plants, such as: aphids, fungi, white flies, mealybugs, and armored scale insects that attack coconut tress.

There are two more bugs that you will want to have as allies in your garden. One is the ground beetle, which is dark brown or black and runs fast. Its shell is striped with lengthwise indentations. Its markings set it apart from the beetles that would do damage to your fruit. They eat various types of caterpillars, which can be helpful. The other bug you will want to see visiting your garden is the praying mantis. Aphids are among the unfriendly pests that the praying mantis feeds on.

Pests come in various sizes and shapes, and some seem to gravitate toward particular fruits or berries. They do different things to different parts of the plant, sometimes even the fruit. Some of them have the name of their victims included in their own names, such as the Raspberry Beetle. For every pest there must be a way to show them the door out of your garden. Included in this list of pests are suggestions for natural, organic means to repel or destroy each type.

Aphids

Aphis gossypii

Aphids are not partial to what type of victims they take. These bugs will attack most types of fruit plants by sucking the sap out of their leaves and  buds. In return, they give your plant viruses.

Signs of their presence include curling leaves, red discoloration, stunted growth, and a black, sooty mold.

Greenflies, blackflies, and wooly aphids are examples of aphids. The wooly aphid sucks sap from the bark and shoots of apple trees.

Repelling aphids

There are several ways to discourage the return of an aphid infestation to your garden:

1. Work the soil vigorously with a rake and tiller between fruit plantings.

2. Rotate patches of sunflowers and milkweeds between fruit crop plantings.

3. Plant flowers that repel aphids around vulnerable plants. Aphid-repellent plants include garlic, chives, anise coriander,

nasturtiums, and petunias. Planting an herb garden that includes these crops may be a natural solution to a problem with aphids.

Beetles

Coleoptera x. (the genus name stays the same but the species name changes, depending on the specific type of beetle)

Contarinia pyrivora — Pear Midge grubs attack the small, undeveloped pear fruit, causing them to blacken and fall off in June.

Byturus tomentosus — Raspberry Beetle larvae damage the ripening fruits of raspberry, blackberry, loganberry, and other soft berry plants. They have the appearance of maggots, which are small, white, and numerous.

Harpalus rufipes — Strawberry Seed Beetles feed on the seeds of strawberries from the outside of the fruit.

Otiorhynchus sulcatus — Vine Weevil grubs (young) feed on the fruit of grapes and strawberries, and they sometimes destroy the plants. Adults eat notches out of leaves at night, but do not cause as much damage.

Repelling beetles

Some types of beetles have fled in response to these tactics.

1. Sprinkle the plants with water and dust them with wheat bran.

2. Create a tea of boiled basil or cedar boughs and spray it on the plants.

3. Spray a solution of 2 tablespoons of Epsom salts dissolved in a gallon of water onto the plants.

4. Plant an herb garden with catnip, garlic, onion, radish, rosemary, rue, or tansy.

5. Keep a few marigolds, geraniums, and nasturtiums close by your fruits and berries.

Borers

Borers belong to the order *Lepidoptera*. The scientific name of the "vine

squash borer," which also attacks fruit plants, is *Melittia calabaza*. They were given their name because of the holes they create in the trunks of their host trees, which weakens the trees so that they cease producing fruit. Adult borers have opaque wings and the young have wings of a thin, clear material that bears black markings. They feed on the wood of the tree, and their prey of choice includes peach, apple, plum, and cherry trees. A favorite site to dig into is the graft union of a rootstock, because it is soft and grants easy access to the inner layers of the trunk. Young trees and those that have suffered from drought are also susceptible to borer attacks.

The damage caused by borers includes blackened areas around the site of the attack. The bark is worn down or absent over large portions of the trunk of the tree.

Repelling borers

Inhibiting the laying of eggs is the key to stopping a borer infestation. Covering the tree in several layers of burlap or newspaper has been reported to suppress the borers' natural inclination to lay eggs, because this type of coating suffocates them. Some gardeners have split the roots and bark of their plants to kill the borers directly. Professionals who have worked with trees have advised administering brown, sandy soil on the site of the attack, which will foster healing on that area of the trunk.

Caspid bugs

Lygocoris pabulinus

Caspid bugs attack apples, currants, and gooseberries by sucking the sap from shoot tips, leaves, and fruit.

Leaves at the shoot tips develop tattered holes. Mature apples ripen with corky discoloration or bumps on their skins.

Repelling caspids

Natural means of keeping caspids in check include:

- Raking around plants to unearth the insects and their larvae.

- Keeping your garden friendly to birds, such as maintaining a bird feeder, will keep them returning to your yard, where they are also likely to spot and eat the caspids.

- Growing a patch of mint in your garden will keep a multitude of pests of various sizes away from your fruits and berries.

Caterpillars

Arctia caja is the scientific name for the garden tiger moth.

As a group, caterpillars are as indiscriminate in their tastes as aphids. They feed in spring on all types of fruit plants. They tatter the edges of buds, leaves, and flower blossoms.

Apple Sawfly caterpillars create tunnels to crawl through small, developing apples, and cause them to fall off the tree in June, instead of in autumn. If any fruit remain on the tree, they usually have a scar in the shape of a ribbon across them.

Gooseberry Sawfly is a more visible vermin than some of the others. It can be up to 1 inch in length, green with black dots, and capable of eating up all the leaves of gooseberry and red currant bushes.

Repelling caterpillars

Planting your fruit near garlic, onion, tomato, tansy, celery, hyssop, mint, sage, rosemary, or thyme is a natural, fragrant, and delicious way of repelling caterpillars from your garden. Make sure you also have some marigolds and geraniums, which are toxic to most pests. You can also apply *Bacillus thuringiensis* (Bt), a species of bacteria that kills caterpillars through the release of an enzyme.

Curculio

Chalcodermus aeneus

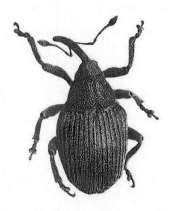

Curculios are small insects that pierce a hole in the fruit as it is forming and lay larvae in it. The fruit will fall prematurely and dark blotches can be seen on fruit that remains attached to its stem.

Grubs

White grubs are called *Cyclocephala spp.*

Grubs are immature caterpillars that bore through young, underdeveloped fruits, and cause them to fall from the tree prematurely. The word grub is also used to refer to the immature stage of many pests. They do more damage than their adult counterparts because they are more voracious.

Repelling grubs

One of the safest means for relieving your plants of the burden of pests is to spray them with liquid that contains a natural toxin to the bugs:

1. Add 3 tablespoons of laundry or dish soap to a gallon of water and spray it on your plants' leaves.

2. Make an extract from pine, poplar, mint, garlic, or hot pepper and spray that on your plants' leaves.

3. *Bacillus thuringiensis (Bt)* is a natural bacterium that is toxic to many pests, if eaten by them. It must be applied during the pests' feeding times.

4. Plant marigolds, geraniums, and nasturtiums near your fruit garden.

Maggots

Lucilia sericata

Maggots are tiny flies that lay their eggs inside fruit, such as apples, which later hatch and render the fruit deformed and inedible.

Apple maggots *(Rhagoletis pomonella)* are the most aggressive of this type of fruit pest, which attacks mature apples. The blueberry maggot attacks blueberries.

Repelling maggots

One method of deterring apple maggots is to place an artificial red apple near your apple tree. They are available at garden stores and are coated with a sticky substance. The shape of the apple attracts the bugs and the sticky coating traps them, so that they do not attack your fruit.

Another decoy that might save your tree is an electric bug-zapping lamp. They are also sold at garden stores and are almost as effective as the artificial apple. Fly maggots are attracted to the light and are destroyed by an electric current run through them by the lamp. A third strategy is clearing the ground of fallen fruit so that pests do not find them attractive sites for nesting.

Mealybugs

Pseudococcus obscurus

This pest is more prevalent on greenhouse-grown plants and sucks the sap of vine fruits and figs. They are mainly white with a pink tint, and appear at the junction of the branch and leaf stem on a plant, covered with a cottony wax.

Repelling mealybugs

A few natural removers of mealybugs from plants can be made at home:

1. Administer a soap spray of 3 tablespoons dish or laundry soap in a gallon of water.

2. Spray an extract of pine, poplar, or mint on the leaves of the plant.

3. Plant marigolds or geraniums close to your fruits and berries.

Mites

Cecidophyopsis ribis — Big Bud Mites usually attack black currants and live in the buds of their trees, which makes them swell into a rounded shape instead of staying narrow and pointed, and fail to develop into leaves, flowers, or fruit in the spring. Their only known victim is the black currant.

Tetranynchus urticae — Fruit Tree Spider Mites are tiny and feed on the sap of apples and plums. They cause yellow spots to appear on the leaves of the plants, which then turn brown and fall off prematurely.

Eriophyes pyri — Pear Leaf Blister Mites attack in May. Their bites leave pale green or pink discoloration on the pear leaves, which turn brown or black later in the year.

Repelling Mites

1. Plant marigolds or geraniums close to plants that are vulnerable.

2. Keep your garden thoroughly weeded and watered.

3. Spray soapy water or plant extract, such as mint, on the leaves of infested plants.

4. Grow asters, geraniums, marigolds, and nasturtiums near your fruits and berries.

5. Include garlic, onions, and thyme, placed close to your fruit plants.

Moths

Cydia pomonell—Codling Moth caterpillars bore holes into mature apples and pears.

Trialeurodes vaporariorum—The Glasshouse Whitefly attacks greenhouse-grown plants. Their usual victims include vine fruits, melons, cape gooseberries, and citrus fruits. The results of their visits are detected in the form of a light green "honeydew" or sooty mold that can be easily dusted off.

Repelling moths

1. Keep an herb garden that includes garlic, mint, onion, rosemary, sage, and tansy.

2. Spray the leaves of plants with soapy water.

3. Grow asters, geraniums, or marigolds to keep the unwanted little bugs away.

4. Hang paper cups that contain a thin layer of molasses at their bottoms to trap codling moths before they have a chance to lay the eggs that produce their larvae.

Nematodes

Radopholus citrophilus

Nematodes are a strand of microscopic cells that together form a parasite that feeds on the roots of your plants. They live their entire lives underground.

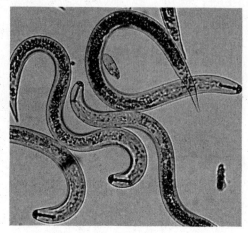

Repelling nematodes

Till organic material into the soil that is also toxic to nematodes. Some of those materials are:

1. Work into your soil a cover crop of timothy, fescue, or ryegrass.

2. Grow repellent plants, such as asparagus, hairy indigo, and calendula.

3. Rotate with brassicas, ground cherry, marigolds, mustard, rutabaga, or watercress for rootknot nematodes. Grow hot peppers or cool watermelon for sting nematodes. Grow beets, radishes, rutabagas, or yams for meadow nematodes.

Pear psylla

This tiny insect works in large groups to attack the leaves of pear trees. They multiply quickly and leave a black, sooty secretion on the plant that ruins fruit crops.

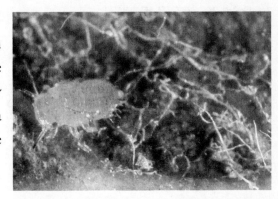

Repelling pear psylla

Cacopsylla pyricola — Attracting their enemies is one way of catching determined pests. Keeping a hedgerow is one way to make your garden inviting to birds. Also, tie black paper to trap the bugs and their larvae before they have a chance to multiply further to help protect your fruit from attacks by these harmful critters.

Scale insects

Hemiptera coccoidea is the scientific name for the "exotic scale insect."

Scale insects possess hard shells that attach to the bark of fruit trees and feed on the sap.

Dactylaspis crotonis — Mussel Scale attacks apples.

Coccus hesperidu — Brown Scale attacks greenhouse-grown vine fruits, peaches, and figs.

Repelling scale insects

1. Spray soapy water on the leaves of the plants.

2. Grow asters, calendulas, geraniums, marigolds, or nasturtiums.

3. Keep an herb garden with garlic, mint, onions, and tansy.

Slugs

Pulmata

Slugs most commonly attack strawberries, damaging the fruit so that it is inedible.

Slug repellents are those used for a variety of other pests, including:

1. Soapy water spray.

2. Pine or mint extract.

3. Herbs such as garlic and onion.

4. Keeping geraniums and marigolds growing close by.

5. Rotating the location of fruit crops each year.

Suckers

Hypostomus plecostomus

Like aphids, suckers attack fruit plants by sucking their sap. Flowers and leaves on apple and pear trees develop a dark, sooty mold caused by drips from the suckers on leaves and twigs, called "honeydew." The mold can be spread by the wind.

Wasps

Vespa vulgaris

Wasps are flying insects with stingers that feed on ripe apples, pears, plums, and grapes.

Hymenoptera — Plum sawflies are the larvae of wasps that create tunnels to crawl through young, underdeveloped fruits on the plum tree.

Repelling wasps

One way to keep wasps at bay is to set a trap for them. This is the way to build it:

1. Set out a bucket of soapy water (3 tablespoons of soap to a gallon of water).

2.   Hang a food that the wasps are attracted to, such as pears, above the bucket.

3.   The wasps will gorge themselves, drop into the bucket, and perish.

Another way to repel wasps is to keep a bed of wild peppermint close to your fruit trees. They avoid peppermint, so you have much less work to do and receive the benefit of fresh mint for your iced tea in the summer. It is best to keep peppermint contained because it is an invasive plant that could spread farther into your garden than you plan to keep it.

Worms

Coleoptera

White grubs feed on the roots of fruit and berry plants, especially those found in forests. They are the larvae of scarab beetles and are C-shaped and wormlike.

Wireworms are the reddish-brown wormlike larvae of click beetles that congregate on the surface of the soil near their victims. The fruits they most often attack are melons and strawberries, when they fall to the ground.

Repelling beetle larvae

There are a number of ways to destroy a population of beetle larvae:

1.   Till the soil in spring, wait two weeks, and weed thoroughly to take away their first food crop of the season, and thus destroy

a larvae colony. This action also unearths them to their natural predators, such as birds.

2. Grow sunflowers to attract them away from your edible crops.

3. Grow onions, garlic, tansy, and thyme near your fruits and berries. They are toxic to pests.

General long-term pest protection

There are a number of strategies you can take to discourage fungi and pests from nesting near your fruit trees and attacking your trees and crops. Together, they amount to keeping your garden clean of debris that are inviting to those pests. Some of the steps you may take include:

1. Pick up all unused fruit and leaves that have fallen to the ground. Add them to your compost pile.

2. Prune your trees regularly and burn the branches.

3. Thin out the branches to allow more sunlight through them to the fruit, and increase the air flow around the tree. This practice will help control the development of mildew and scab.

4. Plant your cultivated fruit trees far away from wild ones and purchase varieties that are resistant to attack from pests and diseases.

5. Plant a large variety of fruit cultivars instead of one type. The variety helps out the honeybees and attracts less notice from pests. This reduces your chances of having your fruit attacked by a vicious bug.

Barriers for keeping out furry scavengers

Protecting your fruit and berry crops from furry little paws is as much work as keeping them safe from attack by colonies of smaller pests. Yet there is one method that is most effective for deterring animals. To keep larger garden thieves away from their crops, some gardeners have installed fences that are taller than the creatures. Some have also added electric wires to the top of those fences as an extra deterrent. Raccoons are the most persistent, but they are usually barred effectively when an electric wire is in use. Other furry taste-testers that can be kept out by this method include mice, rabbits, and deer. In this manner, those fruit and berry growers have been able to secure the majority of their crops for their own use. Clearing the ground of fallen fruit on a regular basis might also discourage them from visiting your fruit garden.

DISEASES

The diseases that attack fruit plants have a number of possible causes. Most of them are preventable with some planning and careful preparation. If you are diligent about keeping the soil your plants are growing in healthy, rotating edible crops at least every other year, and watering them properly, you will be able to avoid many of the diseases mentioned here.

Common causes

Plant diseases usually begin with plants that are neglected in one form or another. Because you would like to have the best start for your fruit-growing adventures, choosing healthy cultivars at the nursery is a very important step. Once you take them home, it is up to you to care for them on a regular schedule of watering and soil enhancement. Mulch materials are very important to the prevention of disease, because they build up important nutrients for all of your fruit trees and bushes.

Light

A lack of light to provide warmth to the plants will prevent them from flowering and producing fruit. Plants that do not receive enough sunshine cannot properly synthesize light into food and energy to grow fruit.

Watering

Plants that do not receive enough water will eventually dry out and die. If that happens, the only thing it will be good for is the compost pile. If you water your fruit trees and bushes too much, there is a risk that the water will cause a fungal disease that attacks the root of the plant.

Fertilization

Fertilizing your fruit tree or berry bush at the wrong time, such as right after the fruit is harvested and before its period of dormancy, may feed pests and diseases that will attack the plant.

Plant and weed competition

Plants that require large amounts of nutrients from the soil are best kept away from the spot in the garden where you have your fruit plants. Otherwise, they may drain the soil of the nutrients you have worked very hard to produce for fruits and berries. The result could be poor quality in the fruit harvested later in the season.

Frost

Frost can cause deep damage to the physical plant, such as a crack. In this crack, fungi and viruses could take up residence, causing havoc to both plants and crops.

Animals

Some wild animals that feast on your fruit plants may carry bacteria that cause diseases that could infect your plants.

Mechanical damage

A lawn mower can damage the trunk of a tree or the stem of a plant, causing it to crack. The crack makes way for diseases and pests to nest and live.

Electrical and septic damage

Electricity and septic system bacteria will burn and damage plants. Make sure your garden is not near a source of electrical energy in order to spare your plants a large amount of distress.

Common types of diseases

Viruses

Viruses are caused by bacteria that multiply underground and destroy plants.

Deficiencies

Deficiencies result from the lack of a vital elemental nutrient needed by your fruit plants. The plants are not receiving the nutrients they need from the soil they are planted in.

Blotches

Blotches are spots on fruit caused by pests. They are often discolored and cause the plant distress.

Blights

Blights are fungal diseases brought upon fruit trees and berry plants by pests.

Examples of common fruit plant diseases

The following diseases are common, and the best defense against them is to use plenty of organic compost, worm castings, and mulch materials. Plenty of sunshine, water, and nutrients are the best offense against them for your fruit plants. If such diseases develop despite your best efforts, the usual course of action is to destroy the infected plants and start all over again. Planting sunflowers is a good alternative as an interim rotation species between two fruit plants. They are lethal for many pests and harmful bacteria.

Anthracnose

Colletotrichum spp.

Grapes are affected by this blight. It is a rot in which spots appear on the fruit, leaves, and new sprouts emerging from buds.

Apple canker

Neonectria galligena

Sunken, discolored patches appear on the trunk of apple or pear trees. Patches of discoloration on the trunk grow longer and become surrounded by arcs of shrunken trunk material surrounding the central patch. *Treatment:* Cut out diseased branches and spurs, and diseased tissue on other branches that have not died.

Brown rot

Monilinia fructigena

The outside of the fruit turns brown and the flesh inside decays. The fruit later develop grayish spores. This disease affects apples, peaches, pears, plums, nectarines, and quinces. *Treatment:* Spread a mix of equal parts borax and sand on the soil surrounding the plant.

Crown gall

Agrobacterium tumefaciens

A giant gall (giant, round mass) develops on cane fruit plants at ground level, with a chain of several more galls further up the canes. *Treatment:* Destroy diseased canes.

Fireblight

Caused by the virus *Erwinia amylovora*

The shoots of apple and pear trees die back. The leaves become withered and fall off. Cankers form and ooze in the spring. *Treatment:* Cut out diseased shoots, plus two feet below that.

Grey mould

Caused by the fungus *Botrytis cinerea*

Strawberries, raspberries, blackberries, currants, and grapes are among many fruits affected by this disease. The

fruit is covered by a grey-brown fluff and rot. *Treatment:* Remove and destroy infected fruit.

Leaf curl and leaf rust

These leaf ailments describe what they look like when attacked by a fungus or virus.

Leaf Curl causes the leaf to curl inward and has spots on it (caused by the plum aphid, *Brachycaudus helichrysi*). Leaf Rust (*Puccinia triticina*)appears as brown or orange spots on the leaf.

Mummy berry

Monilinia vaccinii-corymbosi

This disease attacks blueberries, encasing them in a film that causes them to rot and fall off the branch prematurely.

Reversion

Caused by the virus *Comoviridae*

This disease only affects black currants, and is spread by the "big bud mite". The growth of foliage and fruit is stunted, detected in the smaller mature leaves with fewer veins. Leaves have a magenta color and produce very little fruit. *Treatment:* Destroy all diseased bushes and plant a certified cultivar on a new site, with organic soil.

Silverleaf

"Silverleaf Nightshade": *Solanum elaeagnifolium*

Affects most tree fruits, particularly plums. Leaves turn silver and sometimes turn brown. Buds and branches die back and a purple fungus forms on the dead wood of the branches and trunk. *Treatment:* Destroy the tree if there is dead wood on the trunk. If not, destroy the branches that have been contaminated.

Verticillium wilt

Verticillium dahliae

This is a disease that affects melons. The lower leaves on the plant turn yellow and wilt, after which the whole plant wilts and dies. *Treatment:* Destroy the diseased plants and sterilize the soil.

The following table lists the common pests and diseases for each fruit, according to which plants they attack.

Fruits and the Pests and Diseases that Attack Them

Fruit Species	Common Pests	Common Diseases
Apple	Curculio, codling moth, apple maggot, wooly aphid	Scab, mildew, cedar apple rust
Pear	Psylla, codling moth, pear midge, curculio, stink bug (Asian)	Fireblight, pear scab
Apricots	Curculio, oriental fruit moth	Brown rot
Plums	Curculio, apple maggot, mites, oriental fruit moth	Brown rot, black knot, bacterial spot, Silverleaf
Peaches/Nectarines	Curculio, oriental fruit moth, tarnished plant but	Leaf curl, valsa canker, brown rot, bacterial spot
Melons	Aphids	Verticillium wilt
Strawberries	Strawberry clipper (weevil), strawberry sap beetle, tarnished plant bug	Leaf spot, leaf scorch, gray mold, leather rot, red steele, root rot

Fruit Species	Common Pests	Common Diseases
Blueberries	Aphids, blueberry maggot,	Mummy berry, anthracnose, stem canker
Brambles	Raspberry cane borer, raspberry crown borer, nematodes	Anthracnose, spur blight, cane blight, leaf rust, orange rust, crown gall, raspberry bushy dwarf, raspberry mosaic, raspberry leaf curl, tomato ring spot
Currants and Gooseberries	Caspids,	Reversion (black currants)
Lingonberry	Aphids	Phytophthera root rot (if planted in soil with poor drainage)
Grapevines	Aphids, grape phylloxera, grape flea beetle, grape berry moth, climbing cutworm	Black rot, powdery mildew, Downy mildew, eutypa dieback, phomopsis cane and leaf spot, crown gall, botrytis bunch rot (gray mold), bitter rot, ripe rot, macrophoma rot,
Kiwifruit	Aphids	Actinidia polygama (Silver Vine), Actinidia araguta, actinidia kolomikta,

*Data for this table was obtained from *The Backyard Orchardist* (1993) and *The Backyard Berry Book* (1995), both by Stella Otto, Otto Graphics, Empire, MI.

There are many pests and diseases that you may encounter in the gardening world, but you have control over how you defend your fruits and berries from them. If you have been attending to the land by cultivating the soil with organic compost and mulches and watering your plants often and well, you will be able to bypass the heartache caused by pests and diseases and enjoy a healthy, bountiful harvest when your fruits have ripened. *Read on through Chapter 10 to learn more about when and how it is done.*

CHAPTER 10

Enjoying the Feast — Harvesting and Storing Your Fruit

THE RIGHT TIME FOR HARVESTING TREE FRUIT AND BERRIES

The growing season has flown by with so much to do, and your garden is vibrant with the colors of ripe fruit worthy of a van Gogh painting. Now you have the chance to treat yourself to your favorite fruits and berries, straight from the sturdy branches that hold them. The moment has arrived to grab your sunhat and a bowl and start picking. Maybe you have children to invite to taste the first fruits or berries with you, and they may decide to pick some for you. The first few will probably not make it into any container, but disappear into your mouth. Welcome to the season of harvesting the delicious food you have been laboring for.

The right time to harvest each fruit is when it tastes best. It is soft, but not mushy. The flavor is sweet instead of sour. The skin is firm, yet easy to bite into. The peels of citrus fruit separate readily from the pulp inside. If all of these things are true, you have timed your harvesting well and you have earned a long rest to eat, drink, and bask heartily in your success.

Problems with harvesting too early

You may have tested your fruit for ripeness many times before this day. It may have been pale green, the skin may have been hard, and it may have even smelled unripe, perhaps sour. There is a noticeable difference in how the ripe fruit delights all your senses, and how those senses are activated by an unripe fruit. Because you have been patient, there are many ripe fruits to pick from the tree that all taste scrumptious. Because not all fruits formed by a tree are ripe at the same time, some of those that hang from branches might need more time to be completely ready to eat. But there are some that are eager for you to pick immediately and enjoy.

It is good to be able to determine the difference between ripe and unripe fruit. Unripe fruit deserves the time it takes to develop before it is harvested. Waiting until the right time to pick them, and no more, gives you the opportunity to enjoy the most from the bounty of your plants. If you pick them too soon, they will not be there for you to enjoy later, and they may never reach their full height of flavor. Waiting and watching them develop can be a pleasurable pastime. It will also give you more time to find the best cobbler recipe for baking those peaches or berries.

Problems with harvesting too late

 Waiting too long to pick and eat your fruit can be a problem, too. The more time that passes between the fruit reaching ripeness and the time it is picked increases the chances that the fruit will fall to the ground and rot. This invites pests and diseases to take up residence in your garden, and foragers might enjoy more of the fruits of your labors than otherwise. This will not do after all your painstaking care throughout the growing season. You deserve to enjoy as many ripe plums, pears, and strawberries as you can manage. It is good that there are ways to preserve them all so that you can enjoy them at their peak of ripeness. Freezing and canning them will give you a special treat to look forward to when the harvest season has passed and you are finished gardening for the year. So, go ahead and pick them as they fully ripen, and not a moment later.

METHODS FOR PICKING FRUITS AND BERRIES

The methods for harvesting your bounty vary from one fruit to the next. Small fruits that grow on bushes or vines can be collected in bowls or baskets. Larger fruits that grow on trees may require a ladder and some bushels to collect and contain them. Aside from the vessel into which you place the fruit you harvest, there are unique ways each fruit separates from the branch and allows itself to be picked.

The best way to pick each type of fruit

Brambles

When the fruits of brambles are ripe, they are all plump, sweet, and juicy. Their color stays on your hands and their sweet taste lingers on your tongue. Just make sure you have enough room between bushes so that their thorns

do not linger in your thighs or arms. Raspberries readily separate from the little cap (receptacle) that holds them on the cane, but blackberries and dewberries prefer to keep their caps on when they are taken off. Because they are so small, many of each type will fit into a bowl or basket.

Blackberries, raspberries, and dewberries are eaten in a multitude of ways. They are washed with a dollop of whipped cream over them, whipped into a fool (a creamy pudding made fluffy by egg whites) or baked into cobbler or pie. Smoothies and shakes are also made by combining them with ice cream or yogurt in a blender, and they taste delicious over a bowl of oatmeal or granola. Not only do they taste good, they are full of important vitamins that support the human immune system. Raspberries were used for hundreds of years as an antidote to anemia. Blackberries are great for diabetics to eat because of their natural sweetness, which stays on the tongue and does not raise the blood sugar level.

CASE STUDY: HARVESTING, BAKING, AND PRESERVING RABBITEYE BLUEBERRIES IN NORTH CAROLINA

Connie Stanfield has been growing and harvesting rabbiteye blueberries in Asheville, North Carolina for five years. They are the variety of blueberries that grow well in the Southeastern region of the United States, and she tends 12 bushes of them. Stanfield won 2nd place at the North Carolina Mountain State Fair in 2009 for her blueberry jam.

When asked about the best time to harvest blueberries, she shared that her berries are ready to pick by midsummer. "I harvest them July through August, and sometimes the first two weeks in September," Stanfield said. When they are ready to pluck off the branch, her method of harvesting involves simply picking them by hand and placing them into a plastic bucket.

"When the blueberries are dark blue and plump, they are ripe and ready to pick," Stanfield said. "Unripe blueberries still have pink on them, and they are not as deep blue yet. They are still too firm." Size is not always the best indicator, because even small berries can be ready to pick. "I will pick the very dark berries first, then check lighter ones to see how far along they are."

Stanfield also performs a 'taste test' to check their readiness for harvesting. "Ripe blueberries have a wonderful flavor that bursts in your mouth and melts away. Unripe berries are not as sweet or juicy. They tend to be chewy and quite tart." Yet, sometimes there are blueberries that she does not catch at their peak and they become too mushy. It is too late to harvest those and she leaves them for the birds to eat.

"My favorite part of harvesting is having fresh plump blueberries to eat," Stanfield said. They last 3 to 4 weeks if kept in the refrigerator. She also freezes many of them for later use. "I preserve them in blueberry jam," Stanfield added. She also bakes cobblers, pies, and blueberry bars. The blueberry bars are "everybody's favorite" in her corner of the world. *She has shared her recipe, which appears in Appendix B of this book.*

Strawberries

Ripe strawberries can also be collected in a basket or bowl. They are prolific, so finding the largest vessel to collect them is important. It takes more than 12 months for them to produce ripe fruit that are ready to eat, but when a flush of berries starts to ripen they need to be picked every 2 or 3 days, so that as many as possible are harvested and eaten. The rest can be left to the birds that will make sure no bugs haunt your plants.

Fruit has often been used in a variety of cultures for more than just a sweet snack. Strawberries were used as a medicinal plant by colonial Americans in the 18th century. Teas were made from the leaves and wine from the juice. They were eaten whole and often sprinkled with sugar. The benefits the colonists believed they offered included keeping the teeth white, the eyes free of cataracts, the stomach calm, and the body hydrated in the summer. In the 21st century, they are dipped in chocolate and eaten with whipped cream, or folded into salads, preserves, ice cream, smoothies, and shakes.

Tree fruits

Tree fruits are bigger than berries, so you will need bushel baskets or barrels to collect them. Although they have much in common, such as pits that are ready to plant as soon as they are free of the fruit that hugs them, the rules for harvesting each type are unique.

Peaches will separate from their branch when they are ripe with a gentle twist of the hand. They spoil quickly, so it is best to store your harvested fruit in a cool place, such as a refrigerator, cool basement, or a root cellar. Some favorite ways to eat them over the years include pies, cobblers, compotes, and salads.

Plums are also plucked when they are ripe, sweet, and ready to eat. The blossoms on the tree are powdery. They keep for a few weeks in the refrigerator, but should be eaten or prepared shortly after picking. They have been used to make sweet sauces and preserves, baked in holiday breads and pies, or frozen to eat as a treat in winter. Their juice is sometimes used as a base for punches or fermented to make wine.

Pears need to be picked as soon as they are developed and are easy to twist off the branch, and definitely before they are ripe, without damaging the skin. Wrapping them in tissue paper and storing them in the refrigerator will keep them until they ripen further — about 3 to 8 weeks. When you are ready to eat one, let it sit at room temperature for a few days to bring out the best flavor in the fruit.

Ripe cherries will separate easily from their branch with the stem still attached. They are plump and deep red in color. Although you can crowd a large amount in one container, cherries keep only a short time and should be eaten in some way soon after they are picked. Some of the ways in which cherries have been prepared include baked in pies, juiced, dried (like raisins), canned, frozen, and as the final touch on an ice cream sundae.

photo by Herb Stanfield

Nuts, such as walnuts, almonds, acorns, hazelnuts, and pecans, generally begin falling off the tree when they are ripe and ready to be eaten.

Vine fruits

Grapes are left on the vine until they are plump, sweet, and easily pulled off. They are eaten in bunches off the branch or in salads and sipped as wine or juices. Dried in the sun, they are a favorite childhood snack — raisins.

Kiwifruit have either fuzzy or smooth brown skins that are easily separated from the green pulp inside when they are ripe. They were enjoyed as a treat for hundreds of years in China, and were introduced to New Zealand in the early 1900s. Although kiwifruit are delicious on their own, they are a double treat when paired with a strawberry or tossed in salads. Kiwifruit are also juiced with other fruits in shakes and smoothies. When storing them, they should be kept far from other fruit, because they emit a gas that causes anything else they touch to spoil.

EAT, DRINK, AND SAVE SOME FOR LATER

Before the work of storing some of your harvest to enjoy over the cold winter months, it is time to sit and enjoy them in the way you love best, whether that be sprinkled with sugar, dipped in chocolate, in a salad, floating in a pitcher of sangría, or nestled within a pie crust. No matter how you prepare them, you have earned your right to sit at your table and savor them. Once you have tasted them, you will want to make the party last as long as you can, so you will want to preserve the fruits of your labors in jams or jellies. Other methods of preserving them include canning, drying, and freezing. *A cache of recipes has been provided for you in Appendix B.*

Resources for Finding Garden Tools and Supplies

A fter you have read through this guide, you might still have some questions that refer to specific features in the landscape where you will be planting, or you might want to contact people about subjects that were covered and for which you would like more detailed information. In addition to further visits to your local nursery or other home supply stores, you may also visit the following Web addresses for answers to your questions or to join a gardening forum. You might also have children with whom you would like to share the information in this guide in a way that they would find more accessible or entertaining. You will find all that in the list below, presented according to the subject indicated.

Beekeeping

"BeeCARE": **www.beecare.com**
Hive box construction, bee care, bee care products

"Beemaster.com": **www.beemaster.com/site/honeybee/beehome.
htm** Beekeeping video tutorials and online forums from the Backyard
Beekeepers Association

"Bush Farms": **www.bushfarms.com/bees.htm**
Blog kept by Michael Bush on wholesome, noncommercial,
organic beekeeping

"Massachusetts Beekeeper's Association:" **www.massbee.org**
Provides a directory of those who provide essential beekeeping services

"The Vanishing Bees": **www.vanishingbees.com/beekeeping**
Steps you can take to encourage the re-growth of bee populations

Berries

"Avalon Wine": **www.avalonwine.com/trellising-the-grape.php**
Includes site page illustrating different trellis training designs

"Our Gardening Gang — Growing Bush Berries":
http://ourgardengang.tripod.com/berries.htm
Growing history, habits, and requirements of bramble and bush berries

"Scientific Name Index": **www.ppws.vt.edu/scott/weed_id/rubus.htm**
Growing habits of brambles, under their *Weed Identification Guide*

"The Future is Abundant — A Guide to Sustainable Agriculture":
www.tilthproducers.org/tfia/berries.htm
All of the berries that grow in the Northwest corner of the U.S.

"University of Minnesota Extension":

www.extension.umn.edu/distribution/horticulture/DG2241.html

Development of halfhigh blueberry varieties that will grow in Minnesota and Wisconsin

Buying Healthy Plants

"About.Com":

http://organicgardening.about.com/od/startinganorganicgarden/a/ healthyplants.htm

Plant quality cues to look for when shopping at nurseries

"Kitchen Gardeners":

http://kitchengardeners.org/questions/how-do-i-make-sure-i-buy- healthy-transplants

Useful tips for buying healthy seedlings to transplant, features a page on strawberries

"Suite101.Com":

http://plantsbulbs.suite101.com/article.cfm/how_to_buy_ healthy_plants

Tips for plant cultivar shopping

Citrus Trees

"Citrus 101: How Citrus Trees are Grown":

http://sunkist.com/products/how_citrus_trees.aspx

Steps for all stages of growing a citrus tree

254 The Complete Guide to Growing Your Own Fruits and Berries

"Four Winds Growers":

www.fourwindsgrowers.com/solver/pollination

Growing a variety of citrus trees under varying conditions, including pollination information

City Gardening

"Sustainable and Urban Gardening":

www.sustainablegardeningblog.com

Hosted by Susan Harris, with advice about urban gardening, tools, and many other subjects

(Also, see *Container Gardening*)

Composting

"City Farmer": **www.cityfarmer.org/wormcomp61.html**

A Canadian website about worm composting in an urban environment

"Composting 101": **www.composting101.com**

Full of descriptive details about how to compost organic materials

"Massachusetts State Department of Environmental Protection":

www.mass.gov/dep

Includes designs for composting bins

Container Gardening

"Earth Box — Home Grown Vegetables without a Garden":

www.earthbox.com/consumer/instructions.html

Illustrates the kits designed by this company, and how to assemble them

"Eartheasy": **www.eartheasy.com/grow_raised_beds.htm**
Offers raised beds for gardening in a variety of shapes and materials, with
ideas for use

"Outrageous Gardens": **www.outrageousgardens.com**
Blog about growing fruits and berries in containers, in regions that are
not naturally fertile

Gardening in general

"Do It Yourself Chat Room": **www.diychatroom.com**
A chat room for finding information about any do-it-yourself project,
including gardening

"Finding Dulcinea": **www.findingdulcinea.com**
Online library of resources on a multitude of subjects

"Garden Guides": **www.gardenguides.com**
Has especially useful information about growing dwarf citrus trees
in containers

"Garden Web": **www.gardenweb.com**
Diverse and informative website, forums, articles, etc.

"Global Gardening": **www.globalgardening.org/home/whatis**
Promotes sustainable gardening practices by both individuals and groups

"How-To Garden Guide": **http://howtogardenguide.com**
Growing fruits and vegetables, includes information about organic garden
pest control

"Mid-Atlantic Gleaning Network":

www.midatlanticgleaningnetwork.org/farms.html

Farm dedicated to feeding the hungry with fresh food

"Square Foot Gardening Foundation": **www.squarefootgardening.com**

Hosted by Mel Bartholemew, with information about growing your own fruit

"The Garden Helper": **www.thegardenhelper.com**

Join the gardening forum, have questions answered, find soil testers, etc.

"Transformations": **www.transformations-inc.us/**

Developer of environmentally sustainable homes and communities, both inside and outside

"University of Massachusetts Extension":

www.umassextension.org/nutrition

Gardening, landscaping, and forestry site that covers diverse aspects of growing food

Growing Specific Fruits and Berries

"North Carolina State University Horticultural Information Leaflets":

www.ces.ncsu.edu/depts/hort/hil/hil-208.html

Dedicated to information about growing kiwifruit

"The Rhubarb Compendium":

http://www.rhubarbinfo.com/rhubarb-background.html

Abundant crop of details about the history and use of the plant

"Tradewinds Fruit": **www.tradewindsfruit.com/fruitsscientific.htm**
Lists the scientific names of a wide variety of fruits and berries

"US National Arboretum":
http://www.usna.usda.gov/Hardzone/hrdzon3.html
Maps all the USDA plant hardiness temperature zones

Healing with Fruits, Flowers, and Herbs

"Badger Balm": **www.badgerbalm.com/categories.aspx**
Home of *Badger Balm*™ and other skin healing ointments

"Herbal Beauty":
http://herbalbeauty.blogtells.com/2008/05/26/preparing-tinctures/
Blog with directions for creating tinctures from fruits and flowers for
their healing properties

"Roots and Herbs Farm": **www.laplaza.org/community/rnh/index.html**
Creates organic salves for various purposes, including one named
"Gardener's Salve"

Pests and Diseases

"Featured Creatures":
http://entnemdept.ufl.edu/creatures/beneficial/lady_beetles.htm
A page dedicated to information about ladybugs

"Kearneysville": **www.caf.wvu.edu/kearneysville/wvufarm8b.html**
Fruit tree diseases and their symptoms

Soil Enhancement

"Global Gardening":

www.global-garden.com.au/gardenbegin_soil.htm

Garden soil enhancement strategies

"How to Garden Advice":

www.howtogardenadvice.com/plant_list/fruit/fruit_index.html

Various soil mixes for changing soil pH

"Natural Resources Conservation Service":

www.nrcs.usda.gov/FEATURE/backyard/mulching.html

Abundance of information for improving the quality of garden soil

Soil Testing

"BBC Gardening Guides": **www.bbc.co.uk/gardening/basics/techniques/soil_testingyoursoil1.shtml**

Descriptions and images of different types of soil

"EHow":

www.ehow.com/how_4502045_accurate-garden-soil-test.html

Steps for preparing a soil sample for testing and sending it off to the lab

"European Agricultural Investment Services": **www.eais.net/soil**

Soil types and soil fertility enhancement strategies

"Global Gardening":

www.rain.org/global-garden/soil-types-and-testing.htm

Resource for soil testing steps

"LaMotte Garden Soil Test Kits":

www.biconet.com/testing/LaMGarden.html

Site for ordering soil-testing kits

"University of Massachusetts Extension Labs": **www.umass.edu/soiltest**

Detailed directions for sending a soil test sample to the university labs in Amherst

Tools and Supplies for Gardening

"Freecycle": **www.freecycle.org**

Online community for giving and receiving needed items, free

"Frostproof": **www.frostproof.com/catalog/ht08.html**

Offers a variety of gardening tools and supplies, such as hand tools and grafting tape

"Gardener's Supply Company": **www.gardeners.com/**

All the gardening supplies you could ever need

"Johnny Seeds": **www.johnnyseeds.com/**

Seed-growing supply seller

"Ladder King": **www.ladderking.com/**

A variety of ladders for different purposes

"Peaceful Valley Farm and Garden Supplies":

www.groworganic.com/cgy_458.html?welcome=T&theses=7015515

Sells environmentally sustainable supplies to those who grow organically

"Tree Tie.Com": **www.tree-tie.com/**
Sells a variety of tree ties

"West County Gardener":
www.westcountygardener.com/garden-gloves.php
Sells gloves for different types of gardening for both adults and children

Trees Fruits and Nuts

"Aggie Horticulture":
http://aggie-horticulture.tamu.edu/extension/homefruit
Information about growing tree fruits, including nuts (from Texas A & M)

"EHow":
www.ehow.com/how_2262219_fruit-trees-late-spring-frosts.html
Protecting trees from winter frost damage

"The Heart of New England":
www.theheartofnewengland.com/garden-Nuts.html
Features information about nut growing in New England

"Tree Help": **http://treehelp.com**
Covers all stages and aspects of growing trees, with a directory of arborists

"North Carolina State University":
www.ces.ncsu.edu/depts/hort/hil/ag29.html#pruning
Guide to tree pruning methods

Worms

"Worm-a-Roo": **www.worms.com/worm-a-roo.html**
Sells worms, bins, and worm-related products

"Worm World": **www.agmap.psu.edu/businesses/303**
Raising red worms for composting

"Yuckiest Worm World": **http://yucky.discovery.com/flash/worm/**
Features child-friendly information about worms

"Zephyrus": **www.zephyrus.co.uk/wormhabitat.html**
Detailed information about worms and soil

"North Carolina Water Quality and Waste Management System":
www.bae.ncsu.edu/topic/vermicomposting/pubs/ag473-18.html
Information about vermicomposting

photo by Martin Miller

APPENDIX B

Recipes

A gardening book without recipes would be incomplete. Below are a few for you to try. You may find one here that will make it into your treasure box of favorites. Bon appétit.

APPLE SALSA (Matt Higgins)

Ingredients

3 tart apples (including granny smith or gala, or all of one kind)

3 tablespoons agave nectar

2-3 tablespoons fresh lime juice

½ cup chopped fresh cilantro

½ cup chopped walnuts, almonds, cashews, or macadamia nuts

½ teaspoon ground cinnamon

1. Peel the apples (or not), and core them.
2. Dice them into small pieces, by hand or with a food processor.
3. Place in a bowl with rest of ingredients and mix well.
4. Chill.

BLUEBERRY SQUARES (Connie Stanfield)

Ingredients

1 box butter-flavored cake mix

1 cup rolled oats (not instant)

½ cup brown sugar packed

1 ½ sticks butter, melted and cooled slightly

2 eggs

2 cups fresh washed blueberries tossed with ½-cup sugar

1. Mix cake mix, oats, and brown sugar in large bowl.
2. Add butter and eggs and mix until well blended.
3. This batter is thick. Reserve 1½ cups of batter.
4. Spread rest of batter into greased 9 x 13 cake pan.
5. Top with blueberries.
6. Drop reserved batter over blueberries.
7. Bake at 350 degrees for 40 to 45 minutes.
8. Cool to room temperature. Enjoy fresh or freeze.

CLASSIC SPANISH SPARKLING SANGRÍA

Ingredients

4 (650 milliliters) bottles of red wine

½ cup honey

2 tart green apples, peeled, cored, and sliced

4 sliced fresh peaches

2 bananas, peeled and sliced

2 cinnamon sticks, crushed

3 lemons, cut into thin slices

3 limes, cut into thin slices

3 liters seltzer water

1. Mix all the ingredients together in a pitcher.
2. Place the pitcher in the refrigerator for two hours so that the mix has time to marinate.
3. Pour into tumblers and enjoy with friends.

FRUIT SHAKES

Ingredients

Fruit of your choice

1 cup milk, cream, or vanilla yogurt

1 tablespoon honey or agave nectar

1 teaspoon spice of your choice

Nuts of your choice

1. Toss a handful of frozen sliced fruit or whole berries into a blender. Mix several types if desired.
2. Pour in a cup of milk, cream, or vanilla yogurt.
3. Add a tablespoon of honey or agave nectar.
4. Add a teaspoon of spice, such as cinnamon to an apple shake or cocoa powder to bananas.
5. Add a handful of chopped nuts for texture, such as walnuts to apples or bananas.
6. Blend until smooth.
7. Serve in a tall glass with a straw.

HONEY MADELEINES (a nod to the bees)

Ingredients

7 oz. (1 stick plus 6 tablespoons) butter

3 large eggs

¾ cup sugar

1 teaspoon vanilla extract

⅓ cup milk

2 heaping teaspoons wildflower honey

1 ¾ cups all-purpose flour

2 ½ teaspoons baking powder

1. Preheat oven to 425 degrees Fahrenheit.
2. Heat the butter in a heavy-bottomed saucepan over medium heat until it is golden brown (10-15 minutes).
3. Allow the melted butter to cool slightly before dipping a pastry brush in and lightly greasing the madeleine molds. (e.g. silicone miniature bunt cake molds)
4. Set aside greased molds and remaining melted butter until needed.
5. Mix together the eggs, sugar, and vanilla in a large bowl until smooth.
6. Mix together the milk and honey in a small bowl; when the honey is partly dissolved, whisk it into the egg-sugar mixture.
7. Sift together the flour and baking powder in another bowl.
8. Add the flour mix, a little at a time, to the egg-sugar mixture. Blend each additional spoonful until smooth.
9. Add the remaining melted butter, and whisk vigorously until fully incorporated.
10. Refrigerate for 30 minutes.

11. Fill the prepared madeleine molds almost to the top with batter.

12. Return the rest of the batter to the refrigerator until ready to bake the next batch.

13. Set the molds on a heavy baking sheet.

14. Bake for 12-14 minutes, or until the madeleines are golden brown and have risen, with a crack or bump in the center.

15. Remove madeleines from the mold immediately and allow to cool on a wire rack.

16. Prepare the molds and bake the next batch of madeleines. You may need to melt a little more butter for brushing the molds with before spooning in the batter.

Recipe makes about 20 large madeleines.

HOT APPLE SOUP

Ingredients

1 ½ pound apples

One cinnamon stick

1 thin peel of orange rind

1 ½ cup orange juice

½ to ¾ cup sugar, or 2 tablespoons honey

Lemon juice

1 ¼ cup hot cream

Ground cinnamon to serve

1. Wash, quarter, and core 1 pound of the apples.
2. Put the apples in a pan with the cinnamon stick, orange rind, and 2 ¾ cup of water.
3. Bring the apple and water mixture to a boil and simmer, uncovered, until the apples have disintegrated (about 45 minutes).
4. Rub the mixture through a strainer, discarding the cinnamon stick and rind.
5. Pour the soup back into the rinsed-out pan.
6. Reheat the soup and, when it is halfway to boiling, stir in the orange juice.
7. Sweeten to taste with sugar or honey.
8. Bring to a boil, stirring, and simmer gently for 3 or 4 minutes.
9. Peel and core the remaining apples.
10. Grate the remaining apples into long shreds on the coarsest side of the grater. If the soup is not to be served immediately, squeeze a little lemon juice onto them and toss with a fork.
11. Once the soup has simmered for several minutes, stir in the grated apples and cream.
12. Garnish each serving with either a sprinkling of cinnamon or a few cinnamon croutons. Serves 4.

LEMON MOUSSE

Ingredients

3 large eggs

3 large eggs, separated

1 cup plus 2 tablespoons sugar

2 teaspoons grated lemon zest

½ cup freshly squeezed lemon juice (4 lemons)

Pinch of salt

1 cup heavy cream

Sweet whipped cream

Lemon slices to garnish

1. In a large heat-proof bowl or medium-sized pan, whip the 3 whole eggs, 3 egg yolks, 1 cup sugar, lemon zest, lemon juice, and a pinch of salt.
2. Place the bowl or medium-sized pan over a larger pan of boiling water (or use a double boiler) to cook, stirring constantly with a whisk, for 10-12 minutes — until it is as thick as pudding.
3. Cover with plastic and chill in refrigerator for 1-2 hours.
4. Beat egg whites and a pinch of salt with an electric mixer until they are smooth and white, add 2 tablespoons of sugar, and beat further until they are stiff. Fold the beaten egg whites into the chilled lemon mixture.
5. Beat the whipped cream with 2 tablespoons of sugar and a teaspoon of vanilla extract.
6. Fold cream into chilled lemon mixture.
7. Pour into a serving dish and top with more sweet whipped cream (see #5).
8. Serve garnished with quartered lemon slices. Makes 4 servings.

RASPBERRY FOOL

Ingredients

1 ¼ cups fresh raspberries

¼ cup confectioner's sugar

1 ¼ cups sour cream

½ teaspoon vanilla extract

2 egg whites

Raspberries and lemon balm or mint leaves to decorate

1. Put the raspberries and confectionery sugar in a food processer or blender and blend until smooth.
2. Reserve 4 spoonfuls of the cream for decorative topping.
3. Pour the sour cream and vanilla essence in a bowl and stir in raspberry mixture.
4. Beat the egg whites in a separate mixing bowl until they form stiff peaks.
5. Fold the egg whites into the raspberry mixture.
6. Spoon the raspberry fool into serving dishes and refrigerate for at least 1 hour.
7. Top with a few raspberries, lemon balm, or mint leaves, and a spoon of cream.
8. This recipe may also be used with strawberries or blackberries. Serves 4.

STRAWBERRIES IN CREAM

Ingredients

1 pound ripe strawberries, hulled

Finely grated rind and juice of 1 small sweet orange

6 tablespoons of sugar

1 cup heavy cream

⅔ cup thick vanilla yogurt

1. Place hulled strawberries in a bowl and sprinkle them with orange rind and juice, and a tablespoon of sugar.
2. In a separate bowl, beat the cream until stiff.
3. In a third bowl, beat the yogurt lightly until smooth.
4. Fold the cream into the yogurt with 3 tablespoons of sugar.
5. Fold the strawberries into the cream and yogurt mixture, making sure that all strawberries are completely coated. Add more sugar if necessary.
6. Spoon into individual dessert bowls and chill. Makes 4 to 6 servings.
7. You might also like to use this mix as a topping for fresh buttermilk biscuits.

APPLE PIE

Ingredients

1 refrigerated pie crust

¾ cup all-purpose flour

6 to 7 cups apples cut into thin slices

1 cup white sugar

1 cup brown sugar

1 teaspoon cinnamon

2 tablespoons softened butter

1. Prepare pie crust according to package directions.
2. In a medium bowl combine the apples, brown sugar, and white sugar. Then add the flour, softened butter, and cinnamon. Continue to mix until the apples are well coated.
3. Pour mixture into prepared pie crust. Be sure to cover the edges with aluminum foil to prevent burning or over browning.
4. Bake for 25 minutes. Remove the foil and bake for another 20 to 25 minutes, or until it is golden brown.

FOUR BERRY FRUIT COBBLER

Ingredients

Filling

1 pint strawberries, halved

1 pint raspberries

1 pint blueberries

1 pint blackberries

Zest of 1 orange

Juice of 1 orange

Zest of ¼ lemon

Juice of 1 lemon

¼ cup sugar

2 teaspoons ground cinnamon

5 tablespoons cornstarch

Topping

½ cup butter, softened

1 teaspoon cinnamon

½ cup sugar

2 cups flour

1. Preheat oven to 400 degrees Fahrenheit.
2. Combine all filling ingredients in a large bowl. Mix lightly. This needs to rest for 5 minutes so make the streusel topping.
3. In a medium bowl combine the butter, cinnamon, and sugar. Mix well with a fork.
4. Add flour and mix until topping becomes crumbly.
5. Pour berry filling into a coated 8" x 8"dish and cover with streusel topping.
6. Place in center of cooking grate. Cook 40 minutes or until brown and bubbly.

Recipes makes 6 servings.

GRILLED PEACHES WITH CINNAMON SUGAR BUTTER

Ingredients

1 stick unsalted butter, at room temperature

1 teaspoon cinnamon sugar

2 tablespoons sugar

Pinch of salt

4 ripe peaches

Canola oil

1. Halve and pit peaches.
2. In a small bowl stir butter until smooth.
3. Add the cinnamon sugar, sugar, and salt. Mix well until blended.
4. Heat grill to high.
5. Brush peaches with oil. Place on grill flesh side down.
6. Grill peaches until they are golden brown and just cooked through (3-5 minutes).
7. Top each half with a few teaspoons of the butter mixture.

EASY TRIPLE FRUIT JAM

Ingredients

3 pints fresh strawberries

3 cups superfine sugar

2 tablespoons orange-flavored liqueur

½ Granny Smith apple

½ cup fresh blueberries

1. Place strawberries and blueberries in a colander, rinse, and separate.
2. Cut tops off strawberries and quarter them.
3. Peel, core, and dice the apple.
4. Place the strawberries in a deep, heavy-bottomed pot such as a Dutch oven.
5. Toss strawberries with sugar and orange-flavored liqueur.
6. Bring the mixture to a boil over medium heat. Stir often.
7. Slowly add in the apple and whole blueberries.
8. Continue to keep the mixture at a rolling boil for 25-35 minutes or until the jam reaches 220 degrees on a candy thermometer. Stir occasionally.
9. Skim and throw away any foam that may rise to the top.
10. Allow the mixture to cool to room temperature and then store in a covered dish in the refrigerator.
11. The jam will keep refrigerated for at least 2 weeks. To keep the jam longer, pack and seal in canning jars according to the manufacturer's instructions.

This recipes makes about 3 cups.

FRENCH CREAM FRUIT DIP

1 (8-ounce) package cream cheese, softened

¼ cup granulated sugar

1 cup powdered sugar

1 lemon, zested and juiced

1 cup whipping cream

Pineapple juice

1. Whip softened cream cheese and powdered sugar together until it forms soft peaks.
2. Add in whipped cream, lemon juice, and lemon zest.
3. Continue to beat, adding just enough pineapple juice to achieve desired consistency.
4. Serve immediately with your homegrown fruits and berries or refrigerate for up to a week.

APPENDIX C

List of Scientific Names of Fruits and Berries

Apple,
  Custard apple, *Annona reticulata*
Banana, *Musa acuminata*
Bilberries, *Vaccinium myrtillus*
Blueberries, *Ericaceae* family
  Highbush blueberries, *Vaccinium corymbosum*
  Lowbush blueberries, *Vaccinium angustifolium*
Brambles, *Rubus*
Cantaloupe (Muskmelon), *Cucumis Melo*
Citrus fruits, *Rustaceae* family
Coconut, *Cocos nucifera*
Cranberry, *Vaccinium macrocarpon* or *Vaccinium oxycoccos*

Currant; Gooseberry; Jostaberry, *Ribes*
Grape, *Vitieae*
  European, *Vitis vinifera*
  Fox grape (inc. Concord), *Vitis lambrusca*
  Muscadine grape, *Vitis rotundifolia*
  Sea grape, *Coccoloba uvifera*
Grapefruit, *Citrus paradisi*
Huckleberry, *Vaccinium scoparium*
Kiwifruit, *Actinidia deliciosa*
Kumquat, *Fortunella margarita*
Limes (Key, Mexican, and West Indian varieties), *Citrus aurantifolia*

Lingonberry
("Mountain Cranberry"),
Vaccinium vitis-idaea
Orange, *Citrus sinensis*
PawPaw, *Asimina triloba*
Pineapple, *Ananas comosus*
Rhubarb, *Rheum cultorum*
Strawberries, *Fragaria*
English, *Fragaria vesca*

North American,
Fragaria virginiana
South American,
Fragaria chiloensis
Alpine subspecies,
Fragaria vesca alpina
Sweet Melon (Cantaloupe, Musk,
Winter), *Cucumis Melo*
Watermelon, *Cucurbitaceae family*

photo by Martin Miller

GLOSSARY

Acidic: The presence in soil of too much moisture, indicated by a pH level lower than 7.0. It is caused by low amounts of lime or the application of too much fertilizer.

Alkaline: The presence in soil of too little moisture, indicated by a pH level above 7.0. It occurs in dry, arid climates, such as deserts.

Anther: The male, pollen-bearing part of the stamen.

Apiary: A collection of beehives.

Arbor: A short-latticed trellis for supporting vines.

Arms: The main branches of the grape vine that extend from the trunk. From them extend canes and spurs.

Beveled: Cut or sloped at an angle.

Biennial: Plants or flowers that grow back and bloom every other year.

Bobcat: A machine that is operated in a similar fashion as a backhoe but is wider and built with the means to switch attachments for different purposes. Its wheels are grouped together under a belt so that it will move easily over grass or soil as well as roads.

Bramble: Thorny perennial bushes with erect, arching, or prostrate fruiting branches. The most common examples are the blackberry and raspberry.

Bud: A dormant, undeveloped, compressed shoot. It is formed at the union of the leaf stem with the arm of the vine.

Budwood: Wood from a fruit tree from which a bud will be grafted onto another variety of the same fruit species.

Cane: A mature, woody shoot that still contains buds after a leaf falls off. Also, one-year-old fruiting vine wood.

Canopy: The total complex of leaves and shoots of a grape vine.

Cordon: An extension of the trunk of a grape vine, which usually grows horizontally. From a cordon are usually born arms, canes, or shoots.

Cluster: A group of flowers or fruit that grow and develop from a node.

Crop: Yield of fruit given by a plant.

Cultivar: A variety of fruit tree or berry plant.

Curtain: A portion of the canopy that has had the shoots of a vine positioned according to a particular system of training on a selected trellis.

Day-Neutral Strawberry: A form of Strawberry plant that bears fruit steadily from spring until autumn.

Dolomite: A brittle stone containing calcium magnesium carbonate (Ca, Mg) CO3. Its crystals are usually white to pale pink. Often, it is the stone we refer to as marble.

Floricanes: The branches of a bramble plant that produce flowers and fruit.

Flush: A burst of fruit flowering and production that happens more than once in a season. There are usually periods between each burst when no flower or fruit forms on the plant.

Fruiting Spur: The basal section of a (grapevine) cane, pruned back to bear less than six buds.

Graft: A shoot of one plant that is inserted into another to create a new tree.

Hand Pollination: A form of artificial pollination that involves brushing pollen off flowers that produce it in abundance and brushing it onto those that do not.

Head: The top of a grapevine trunk, including the upper arms.

Heeling-In: Temporarily laying a plant at an angle and burying the roots to hold it until it is planted in the ground. It can be done without taking the plant out of the pot you purchased it in.

Humus: Dark soil that is made up of decayed leaves, rotting wood, seeds, and decayed plants and animals.

Internode: The section between the nodes of the shoot or cane of a grapevine's arm.

Lateral: The shoot or cane borne at the side of an arm of a grapevine.

Legumes: Plants in the bean family, including peanuts, chickpeas, and split peas.

Lime: Ground limestone applied to soil in order to raise its pH level.

Muscadine Grapes: A type of grape that thrives only in the temperate climates of the Southeastern states.

Nematode: Worm-like parasite that feeds on tree roots.

Neutral: The quality of soil with a pH between 6.0 and 6.8. There is a balance of nutrients and moisture present in the soil.

Node: The thick part of the shoot of a grapevine where the leaf and bud are located.

Nursery-mature: Plants that have grown in the ground for a few months at a nursery in order to acclimate them for growth in an outside garden and to prepare them for the rigors of transplanting.

Ovary: Part of the green base of the flower blossom where fruit and seed are produced.

Ovule: The part of the flower located in the receptacle that develops into a seed.

Parthenocarpic: Pertains to fruit flowers that are not pollinated and thus bear fruit without seeds.

Parthenogenesis: Sexual reproduction without fertilization.

Perennial: Plants or flowers that grow back and bloom every year without the need to be replanted.

Pergola: An arbor with a latticework roof.

Perlite: An acidic, glassy rock that takes the form of round crystals, with the same chemical makeup as obsidian.

Photosynthesis: The process by which trees convert the light of the sun into food and energy for growth and development.

Picking Tool: A long pole with a basket attached at the top, designed for harvesting tree fruit.

Pistil: The small tendrils in the middle of a flower or plant that carries the seeds.

Pollination: The process by which pollen is put on the pistil of a plant.

Pollinator: A fruit tree or berry plant that produces enough pollen for cross-pollination with others.

Pollinating Variety: A fruit tree or berry plant variety that is able to produce enough pollen for cross-pollination with other varieties of the same species.

Polythene: Shortened version of Polyethylene, a type of thin, flexible plastic.

Primocanes: The branches of a bramble plant that do not produce flowers or fruit.

Receptacle: The bottom of a flower bud that holds together all the reproductive organs, and from which the seeds for pollination emerge.

Renewal Spur: The cane of a grapevine cut back to contain one or two buds, meant to replace and renew an older cordon or spur.

Rootstock: The roots and a few inches of trunk above that.

Royal Jelly: A substance secreted from the heads of female nurse bees, filled with special nutrients for feeding the larvae in the eggs that the queen bee lays.

Runner: The offshoot a "parent" plant is expected to create, from which future cultivars are taken, and from which future fruit crops are expected to grow.

Scion: The trunk, branches, leaves, and fruit of a tree.

Shoot: The green growth that originates from an arm, bud, cane, cordon, spur, or trunk of a grapevine in the spring. It always bears leaves, and may also bear fruit.

Soil Plug: The soil surrounding the roots of a plant that has been cultivated for transplanting.

Softwood: Wood taken from a fruit tree or plant in early summer, when it is growing most vigorously.

Spermatheca: An organ in the queen bee where the sperm from the drones she mates with are kept until they are used to fertilize eggs that will become either female worker bees or future queens.

Stigma: The tip of the pistil — the female, pollen-receiving part of the flower.

Subsoil: The layer of soil found beneath the topsoil.

Sucker: A grapevine shoot that develops from a bud that originates underground.

Temperate: Mild or moderate, with no extremes of hot or cold weather.

Tendril: A twining, curly grapevine shoot that holds to anything it touches, and occurs opposite a leaf.

Tissue-Cultured: Plant cultivars that are propagated with live, growing plant tissue; transplanted while they are actively growing instead of dormant.

Topsoil: The top, dark, nutrient-bearing layer of soil.

Trunk: The vertical stem of a grapevine that grows vertically above the ground. There may be more than one trunk grown by a vine.

Vermicomposting: The process by which worms are used to break down your kitchen scraps.

Vermiculite: A smooth, glassy rock with markings that look like worms.

Vigor: The rate and volume of growth produced by a grapevine.

Vine Size: The weight of the vine growth pruned away from a grapevine.

Windward: Toward (or in) the direction from which the wind blows.

AUTHOR BIOGRAPHY

photo by Sarah Florreich

Karen Szklany Gault spent her childhood in Hawthorne, New York and has since called Ireland and several of the United States her home. She holds a B.A. in Psychology from Marist College (1986) and a M.Ed. in Elementary Education from the University of Massachusetts, Boston (1996). She currently resides in Berlin, Massachusetts with her husband and daughter as a member of Mosaic Commons, a cohousing community, where she enjoys creating her own backyard garden and home-schools her daughter, Cosette. When she is not gardening or home-schooling, she makes music, walks labyrinths, sails, cooks, bakes, and makes cross-stitch tapestries.

photo by Martin Miller

INDEX

A

Acidic, 41, 43, 60-62, 83, 97, 100, 141, 145, 148, 151, 156, 170, 173, 197, 279, 281

Alkaline, 41, 60, 61, 62, 63, 65, 67, 80, 186, 197, 279

Aerate, 86

Amended, 63, 67

Anthracnose, 233, 238, 239

Anther, 113, 279

Apple canker, 234

Arbor, 166, 279, 281

Arm, 14, 35, 169, 279, 280, 282

Artificial pollination, 102, 112, 115, 116, 117, 280

B

Backhoe, 96, 97, 279

Bark mulch, 76, 78, 84, 131, 136

Beveled, 95, 279

Biennial, 279

B (continued)

Blight, 234, 239

Boiler, 269

Bramble, 20, 38, 48, 54, 100, 104, 140, 142, 143, 198, 201, 252, 279, 280, 281

Brown matter, 81

Brown rot, 234, 238

Budding tape, 97, 126

Budwood, 125, 279

C

Cane, 20, 21, 50, 169, 235, 238, 239, 244, 279, 280, 281, 282

Canopy, 38, 165, 168, 172, 200, 208, 279, 280

Castings, 41, 54, 63, 68, 70-74, 88, 199, 233

Compost, 42, 48, 54, 64, 66, 67, 69, 71-74, 79, 80, 82, 83, 85-88, 94, 95, 123, 130, 133, 138, 148, 160, 163, 186, 187, 199, 209, 229, 231, 233, 239, 254

Cold frame, 102, 137

Colony Collapse Disorder, 117, 120

Container, 26, 27, 43, 44, 54, 58, 59, 70, 73, 79, 99, 124, 134, 137, 148, 155, 164, 177-180, 183, 184, 186, 187, 195, 212, 242, 248, 254

Cordon, 167, 168, 279, 280, 281, 282

Crop, 19, 23, 24, 28, 39, 41, 46, 51, 63, 76, 77, 86, 87, 112, 147, 154-156, 171, 214, 224, 228, 256, 280

Cross-pollination, 111-113, 115, 116, 133, 148, 149, 171, 182, 190, 281

Crown, 129, 159, 173, 174, 212, 235, 238, 239

Crown gall, 235, 239

Cultivar, 20, 21, 48, 54, 97, 103, 124, 135, 154, 183, 212, 237, 253, 280

Curtain, 168, 280

D

Deficiency, 212

Dormancy, 26, 27, 43, 51, 162, 192, 201, 205, 206, 207, 231

E

Ecosystem, 18, 22, 25, 32, 33

Electric heater, 191

End posts, 166, 167

F

Fan system, 169

Fertilization, 110-114, 231, 281

Filament, 113

Fireblight, 235, 238

Floricane, 141, 143

Flush, 155, 246, 280

Four Arm Kniffen, 169

Frost pocket, 44, 162

G

Gas heater, 191

Germinate, 76, 101, 110, 138, 194

Grafting, 98, 100, 116, 124, 125, 259

Greenhouse, 20, 25, 34, 44, 102, 117, 138, 175, 177, 178, 186-195, 212

Green manure, 77

Green matter, 81

Grey mould, 235

H

Hand pollination, 116, 117, 140, 280

Harvesting, 50-53, 88, 104, 106, 187, 241-247, 281

Haws can, 99

Head, 90, 95, 113, 120, 130, 169, 191, 280

Heeling-in, 164, 280

Hill system, 157

Humus, 75, 76, 82, 83, 280

Hybrid, 23, 29, 147, 168

L

Leaf Curl, 236, 238, 239

Leaf Rust, 236, 239

Line posts, 166, 167

Low-chill, 27, 29, 148

M

Macroclimate, 21, 22

Manure, 61, 67, 74, 77, 79, 81, 84, 85, 138, 174, 199

Matted-row system, 157

Mummy Berry, 236, 238, 239

N

Nectar, 18, 46, 110, 112, 118, 119, 263, 265

Nematode, 280

Neutral, 41, 60, 62, 63, 76, 80, 163, 197, 280

Nightshade, 237

O

Ovaries, 113

Ovules, 109, 110, 113

P

Paraffin heater, 191

Parthenocarpy, 114

Parthenogenesis, 114, 281

Peat moss, 53, 61, 70, 71, 83, 84, 135, 148, 151, 174, 204

Perennial, 20, 21, 141, 173, 279, 281

Pergola, 281

Perlite, 83, 84, 281

Pest, 44, 255, 163, 212, 213, 220, 221, 229

pH level, 41, 58, 59, 61, 75, 83, 279, 280

Photosynthesis, 44, 198, 281

Pistils, 109-112, 114, 116, 171

Pollen-producer, 102, 115, 116

Pollination, 45, 102, 108, 109, 111, 112, 114, 115, 116, 117, 118, 119, 120, 121, 137, 139, 140, 198, 203, 254, 280, 281

Pollinating variety, 113, 115, 281

Pollinator, 110, 111, 115, 117, 281

Porous, 62

Potash, 74

Power rake, 97

R

Raised bed, 54, 103

Receptacle, 109, 113, 244, 281

Reversion, 237, 239

Root girdling, 187

Rootstock, 97, 100, 125, 126, 127, 134, 163, 173, 216, 281

Runner, 156, 282

S

Sand, 22, 27, 32, 62-67, 70, 73, 80, 81, 83, 84, 85, 91, 97, 107, 141, 234

Sap, 76, 205, 211, 214, 217, 221, 222, 225, 227, 238

Scion, 97, 100, 124-126, 282

Self-pollinating, 46, 110, 111, 113, 146, 156

Shoot, 169, 172, 202, 217, 279, 280, 281, 282

Silverleaf, 237, 238

Soil, 18-21, 23-27, 29-31, 33, 34, 38, 40-43, 48, 53-55, 57-88, 92, 94-97, 100-103, 106, 110, 123, 124, 127-139, 141, 142, 144-146, 148-153, 156-160, 163-165, 170-174, 178, 180-184, 186, 187, 190, 194, 195, 19-200, 204, 205, 207, 208, 212, 213, 214, 217, 224, 228, 230, 231, 233, 234, 237, 238, 239, 256-259, 261, 279-282

Soft rot, 139

Softwood, 94, 282

Soil plug, 123, 144, 148, 282

Spaced-matted-row system, 157

Spade, 57-59, 81, 95, 123, 129, 195

Sphagnum moss, 84

Spur, 169, 239, 280, 281, 282

Stamen, 112, 113, 279

Stigma, 16, 109, 112, 113, 282

Style, 13, 19, 53, 98, 113

Subsoil, 82, 282

T

Temperate zone, 137

Tissue-cultured plant, 282

Tree fruit, 21, 23, 27, 28, 106, 114, 133, 172, 200, 241, 281

Tree guard, 135

Tree nut, 21, 23

Trellis, 252, 21, 28, 39, 50, 53, 165, 166, 167, 168, 169, 172, 182, 200, 201, 203, 279, 280, 10

Trunk, 52, 124, 126-129, 131, 150, 167-169, 171, 198, 202, 204, 206, 209, 211, 216, 217, 232, 234, 237, 279, 280-282

Topography, 40, 41

Topsoil, 82, 83, 85, 131, 282

V

Vermicomposting, 69, 72, 261, 282

Vermiculite, 83, 84, 282

Verticillium wilt, 238

Virus, 60, 235, 236, 237

W

Worm bin, 68, 70, 72, 73